Milestones in the New Testament

An Examination of Key Passages

Bob Evely

To

Our amazing grandchildren,

Seven thus far.

You bring so much joy into our lives,

And we cherish every moment we have together.

May God bless you beyond measure,

All the days of your lives!

With love,

Grampa & Grandma

"Trail Guides"
Elinor Evely (Nov. 2018)

"Trail Guides"
Allison Evely (Nov. 2018)

Milestones in the New Testament

An Examination of Key Passages

Bob Evely.

Copyright 2018, Robert W. Evely, Wilmore KY

*Scriptures taken from the Concordant Literal New Testament
and the Concordant Version of the Old Testament unless otherwise noted.
Concordant Publishing Concern, 15570 West Knochaven Road,
Santa Clarita, CA 91387 (www.Concordant.org)*

Grace Evangel Fellowship:
P O Box 6, Wilmore, KY 40390
www.GraceEvangel.org

Writings; Milestones in the New Testament, An Examination of Key Passages
by Bob Evely
Copyright © 2018 by Robert W. Evely

All rights reserved. This book or any portion thereof may not be reproduced or used in any manner whatsoever without the express written permission of the publisher except for the use of brief quotations in a book review or scholarly journal.

First Printing: 2018

ISBN 978-1-7323228-4-4

Cover created by Cris Evely
Front: The Evely girls with friend Violet
Back: "Trail Markers" by Allison Evely

Published by:
Robert W. Evely
P.O. Box 6
Wilmore, KY 40390

www.GraceEvangel.org

Table of Contents

Opening Remarks	5
Milestones in the Gospels	9
Milestones as they awaited the King's Return	65
Milestones in Paul's Ministry	95
Milestones in Revelation	241

Opening Remarks

When one observes a forest from afar, he gets a much different perspective than if he closely examines each individual tree in the forest.

A study of the Bible can be viewed in the same way. One can observe the forest ... noting the broad overarching flow of the Scriptures to understand how it all fits together and is to be interpreted. Or one can observe individual trees ... individual passages found within the Scriptures.

This study will be an attempt to find the middle ground. We will walk thru the forest (the Bible) and will stop to observe the most revealing trees; the key passages in the Scriptures that set the tone for the Bible as a whole.

To Facilitate Discussion

A more detailed overview of the New Testament can be found in my previous four books.

The Visitation (The Gospels)
The Waiting (Acts Part 1 and the Circumcision Letters)
The Pause (Acts Part 2 and Paul's Letters)
The Return of the King (Revelation)

This present work covers the same ground as all of the above, but in a much more abbreviated fashion. And the format is designed primarily to facilitate discussion.

That is my purpose here ... to facilitate discussion. Each stopping point is followed by a few brief comments; after which I encourage you to think and discuss with others.

Rightly dividing

Endeavor to present yourself to God qualified, an unashamed worker, correctly cutting the word of truth (2 Timothy 2:15). In most translations *correctly cut* is translated *rightly divide*.

We must pay close attention to the context. To whom is God writing? Does the passage pertain directly to us in this present era, or was God working differently in that previous era, and perhaps with a different people group?

It is certainly true that *all scripture is inspired by God and is beneficial for teaching, for exposure, for correction, for discipline in righteousness, that the man of God may be equipped, fitted out for every good act* (2 Timothy 3:16). But this does not mean that all scripture is speaking directly to us in our present-day context.

For example, if God speaks to those of Israel in a past era and context; we cannot force that passage to apply to our present situation. God is always the same God, but by His choice and to fulfill His purposes He has chosen to work differently in different eras.

Rightly dividing God's Word is a divine precept on the same level as all other of God's instructions. If we fail to rightly divide, confusion will reign and it will not be possible to understand that which God has revealed.

For example, when we read; *Go not into the way of the Gentiles ... but go rather to the lost sheep of Israel* (Matthew 10:5-6); we might think this is in conflict with other passages that command disciples to go into all the world. But both are words of God and both must be true. We cannot simply discard one and retain the other, and we cannot allow one truth to upset another truth. The only solution is to "rightly divide" the word of God. One passage announces God's plan in one era, and the other shows how God is working at a later time.

The New Testament

It seems that the New Testament can be divided into four distinct parts.

The Visitation consists of the four gospel accounts that document the Lord's life and ministry upon the earth.

The Waiting (or "The Fellowship of Jewish Believers") consists of the first part of Acts and the letters written by the Jewish apostles and leaders to the ecclesia which then consisted exclusively of believers *among Israel*. These believers are encouraged to persevere and endure as they face persecution and trial, and as they await the return of their king to reign upon the earth in the restored kingdom.

The Pause (or "The Fellowship of All Believers") consists of Paul's ministry; the second portion of Acts as Paul is commissioned as a 13th apostle and as he receives new revelation from God and a new commission; and Paul's letters that contain this new revelation. This is especially true of his later letters. We will see a distinction even within Paul's letters, with his early ministry directed to Israel first and only to the nations when he is cast out of the synagogues in various locations ... and his later ministry that announces *secrets* concealed by God in times past and now revealed; and with the nations of equal stature with Israel. Here we see a pause in God's workings with Israel, His chosen people. Paul's writings are parenthetical proclamations during the pause. Israel is temporarily set aside to the benefit of the nations (Romans 11:25). Paul introduces new things that had been a *secret* (by God's choosing) in times past. For the first time God reveals thru Paul the Body of Christ; *called-out-ones* not just from among Israel but from among all nations. Those of the nations are joint heirs with no preference given to those of Israel, which had been the case in the past. The Body of Christ does not await Christ's return to reign upon the earth. Instead the expectation is for Christ to call the Body into the heavenly realm (1 Thessalonians 4:13ff).

<u>The Return of the King</u>. The book of Revelation records the events leading up to and culminating with the return of the king to reign in the restored kingdom upon the earth.

Think for yourself!

I challenge you to think for yourself as you study the Bible! Theologies are nothing more than <u>theories</u> to be challenged and tested to be sure they are correct. Don't simply accept the theology that has been handed to you by your church or your pastor. Test it! Study and think for yourself.

If you think that your church, pastor or Bible teachers are correct in their understandings and teachings, consider this. Near the end of Paul's life nearly all had abandoned him and his teachings, and had turned away from truth. Near the end of Peter's life the same was true. At what point in history after their deaths do we think that church leaders and the majority within the church got it right?

I contend that the church <u>remains</u> in apostasy, and church leaders are being used by the Deceiver to cloud and distort the truth, and this is evidenced by the many different churches teaching significantly different things.

So I am simply asking you to study and to think for yourself. The overviews I have prepared on the New Testament represent my own perspectives. I don't claim to be right on all specifics and that everyone holding other views is wrong. I study the evidence and I think, and contained herein are my *theories* to be considered and tested.

You have been taught what the Bible means, and this has become the *theory* you now hold to be true. Challenge that theory. Examine the facts and evidences and consider that your theory (and that of your "experts") might be wrong on some points. Open your Bible and study anew. Think for yourself!

Setting the stage for Matthew's account

As we prepare to start our New Testament overview, consider the events that unfolded throughout the Old Testament that set the stage for Matthew's account.

God had established a kingdom upon the earth for His chosen people, the Israelites. As king of Israel, David brought unity and power to this kingdom. He was followed by Solomon, under whose reign the kingdom increased its borders and lived in peace.

But after Solomon the kingdom declined sharply. Eventually both the northern portion of the kingdom (Israel) and the southern portion (Judah) were conquered, and the people were led away into exile.

But there remained a light! Through the prophets God assured the people they would one day be returned to the land; and in fact they were. The temple was rebuilt, as were the walls of Jerusalem.

As Matthew opens the people are back in their land, but it is not *their* land and they are not in control. The Roman government rules over Israel and it has been 400 years since the last of the prophets had spoken. The people await a further word from their God.

So in accord with Old Testament prophecies, Israel is waiting and watching for the restoration of the kingdom. They await their king; the Messiah. It is with this anticipation that Matthew begins.

Milestones in the Gospels
"The Visitation"

An Overview of the Scriptures, by
BOB EVELY © *2018.*
An Independent Minister of Christ Jesus,
Of the church at Wilmore, Kentucky

Let us now begin our walk thru this wonderful forest; the New Testament Scriptures. While we have titled this study "milestones," perhaps a more appropriate term as we stop at the "trees" of interest might be "trail markers."

Matthew

The four gospel accounts that open the New Testament can be labelled "The Visitation," as they provide an account of our Lord's visitation to the earth. We note that Luke comments, *"You knew not the era of your visitation."* (Luke 19:44)

Matthew opens with the lineage of Jesus; important since a large part of Matthew's purpose in writing is to document that the qualifications are met for Jesus to be the Son of David, the King, the Messiah.

Prophecies are fulfilled in the birth of Jesus, and many Old Testament references are provided by Matthew throughout to record fulfillments of these prophecies by Jesus.

Immediately after the Lord's birth account, Matthew turns to John the Baptist. John is proclaiming a message we will see repeatedly and consistently throughout the gospel accounts, *"Repent! For near is the kingdom of the heavens."*

To the Pharisees and Sadducees that gather, John's message is not so pleasant: *"Who warns you to flee from the impending indignation."*

++

Let us stop at our first trail marker.

> ### Trail Marker #1
> ## The Kingdom is Near (3:2)

David's kingdom was ordained by God and established upon the earth. The prophets would later speak of a restoration of that kingdom, with a successor king from David's line.

Early in Acts the apostles asked if this kingdom was about to be restored, so that continued to be the expectation of believers among Israel ... the kingdom's restoration upon the earth. We will see this restoration when Christ returns in Revelation.

But for now ... the kingdom is near.

Milestones in the Gospels *(The Visitation)*

++ Some observations along the way ++

Jesus is tempted, and He prevails. This is an interesting parallel to Adam who was also once tempted, but he failed. Christ, the second Adam, represents humanity ... and He overcomes temptation.

Jesus proclaims the evangel of the kingdom using the same words as John the Baptist: *Repent! For near is the kingdom of the heavens.*

Jesus calls His disciples and leads them thru all of Galilee ... teaching in the synagogues, heralding the evangel of the kingdom, and healing. (4:23)

We come to our next observation point ...

> ### Trail Marker #2
> # Teaching, heralding, healing
> (4:23)

The strong connection between teaching, heralding, and healing seems to make sense, since Christ was directing His words exclusively to Israel whose expectation was upon the earth.

In accord with the prophets, Israel awaited the Messiah to return and to restore the kingdom upon the earth with a king of the line of David. Israel's blessings were always upon the earth, the land, and physical blessings in response to obedience.

But the Body of Christ has its expectation in the heavens. We have a celestial destiny and a celestial expectation; and grace is sufficient! Can we therefore expect that the same teachings and healings apply to us as they did to Israel in that day?

All we know from this account in Matthew is that there is a relationship between teaching, heralding, and healing during this time when Jesus is proclaiming the evangel of the kingdom to Israel.

Today we have no expectation of a physical land. We await the Lord to snatch us away into the heavens, (1 Thessalonians 4:13ff) not to come and establish the kingdom here upon the earth. That is Israel's expectation, and it makes sense that a message concerning things to occur upon the earth would be accompanied by signs such as healing that have an effect in life upon the earth.

This is not to say that God will no longer bring supernatural healing in some instances. I am simply suggesting that the connection we see in Matthew between teaching, heralding and healing no longer seems to be pertinent as we proclaim a different evangel; the evangel of peace, reconciliation, and grace that has been charged to us in this present era.

God is always the same God, but He chooses to work in different ways in different eras.

++ Some observations along the way ++

Throngs follow Jesus, bringing to Him all who have illnesses and torments.

In chapter 5 we see the "Beatitudes." Rewards are to come in the kingdom for those who are poor, who mourn, who are meek, who are hungering for righteousness, who are merciful, who are clean in heart, who are peacemakers and who are persecuted. The rewards will be consolation, an allotment of the land, satisfaction, mercy, the ability to see God, the right to be called sons of God and vast wages.

Some of these rewards, especially <u>an allotment of the land</u>, show us that the expectation at that time is the kingdom to come upon the earth, and not "heaven." We have no right to spiritualize these words of Jesus, causing the kingdom to become heaven. It is real land upon the earth that is to be enjoyed by Israel when the kingdom is restored.

Now let's pause for a moment at another interesting observation point …

Trail Marker #3
The Sermon on the Mount (5:1)

Let me suggest that "The Sermon on the Mount" might better be called "Rules for the Kingdom." These words can certainly convey principles for us to remember today, but we must be careful as to how we *apply* them.

Remember that Jesus is speaking to the Jews of His day, getting them ready to live within the kingdom when it is restored upon the earth. We cannot assume that things stated to the Jews of this particular era will automatically apply to non-Jews in the 21st century.

Could it be that these "kingdom rules" are requirements that cannot possibly be fully observed by any man?

Could it be these requirements were given to show man his incapability to enter the kingdom thru self-righteousness and works, and that full dependence on Christ is needed?

When Christ does return could it be that what we read in Revelation is describing a process for preparing man to enter the kingdom?

++

Now another brief stop along the way ...

> ## Trail Marker #4
> ## Gehenna (5:22)

The Greek word *gehenna*, translated *hell* in most English translations, is first mentioned in Matthew 5:22. But is Gehenna really "hell" as most Bible translations would have us believe?

It is the Greek form of the Hebrew *Gai Hinnom* or *Valley of Hinnom*. This is a physical place; a ravine just below Jerusalem. This place is referred to in 2 Chronicles 28:3 and 33:6. In Jesus' day it was a refuse dump with fires perpetually burning.

When Jesus talked about *Gehenna* his audience understood that He referred to this refuse dump outside of Jerusalem. For certain crimes once the kingdom is restored, the bodies of the guilty will be cast into this place; a disgraceful fate. Isaiah 66:22-24 foretells this, and the terminology used shows that it is clearly a physical and not a spiritual location. *All flesh* will see the corpses of the *mortals* burning in the fire as they come to Jerusalem to worship.

This was Jesus' first reference to *Gehenna*. Had He been referring to a spiritual place of endless torment, something far different from the *Valley of Hinnom* that the Jews were familiar with, this would have been a new concept and many questions would have been asked and clarifications needed.

From Genesis forward the penalty for sin is death, not endless torment. If Jesus is changing the penalty to endless torment, surely He would have provided further explanation as to this change.

> **Trail Marker #5**
> # The Lord's Prayer (6:9)

Chapter 6. The Lord's Prayer. Jesus' words speak of a kingdom *to come upon the earth as it is in heaven.*

Those of Israel that Jesus is addressing do not have an expectation of "going to heaven," but instead that the kingdom will come upon the earth.

While this prayer is repeated weekly in many of today's churches, it is really a prayer intended for Jewish believers in Jesus' day. The expectation of the Body of Christ is to be called upward to be with the Lord and to serve Him there, in the celestial realm.

Milestones in the Gospels *(The Visitation)*

++ Some observations along the way ++

Chapter 8. Miracles again accompany the evangel. A leper is healed, and a centurion's son, and Peter's mother-in-law. MANY are healed and demons are cast out. The sea is calmed. Two demoniacs are healed.

More in chapter 9. A paralytic is healed, and a dead girl is raised. A woman with bleeding is healed, as well as two blind men. Demons are cast out of a mute demoniac.

With all of these signs and wonders we pause for another milestone to consider a point of disagreement among believers today ...

> ## Trail Marker #6
> ## Are miracles to be expected in our present day?

Healings and other miracles were prevalent in these days as the kingdom evangel is being proclaimed. We previously observed the close relationship between proclaiming the kingdom evangel and miracles. It seems that miracles were one of the MEANS used to proclaim the kingdom.

But this does not necessarily mean that miracles will continue to be the norm in later eras, as when Paul later proclaims the evangel entrusted to him.

This is not to say that God could not perform miracles even in our present day; most certainly He can. But could it be that miracles served a purpose in proclaiming the kingdom evangel which was focused on earthly blessings for Israel, that is perhaps not served in Paul's message that *grace is sufficient*.

Milestones in the Gospels *(The Visitation)*

++ Some observations along the way ++

Back to Matthew; chapter 9.

Criticism. Some of the scribes criticize Jesus for pardoning the sins of the paralytic. He is criticized for eating with sinners. John's disciples ask Jesus why His disciples do not fast.

Jesus notes the cause of their criticism; they are putting fresh wine into old wine skins. Jesus is bringing new teachings and they are not fitting the old understandings.

More miracles. Jesus raises a girl that had died. He heals a woman that had a hemorrhage for twelve years. Two blind men are healed, as well as a mute demoniac.

And again we see the relationship between teaching, heralding, and healing as Jesus goes about all the cities and villages doing so.

Chapter 10. Jesus calls His twelve disciples and prepares to send them out to heal and rouse the dead and cast out demons.

++

We reach our next stopping point ...

> ## Trail Marker #7
> ## They are to go only to the lost sheep of Israel (10:6)

The Twelve are to herald the message, *Near is the kingdom of the heavens* ... BUT ONLY TO ISRAEL.

To ignore the context provided in the Scriptures and to apply things to ourselves that were given to Israel is STEALING. And doing so causes us to misunderstand the revelation God has provided to us in His Word.

We cannot claim, at least not from this passage, that our commission is the same today. This commission was given to a specific group of people at a specific time and for a specific purpose.

Milestones in the Gospels *(The Visitation)*

++ Some observations along the way ++

Chapter 11. Once Jesus had finished commissioning the Twelve, He continues with His own teaching and heralding.

John the Baptist sends his disciples to Jesus asking, *Are You the One?* Instead of a direct response, Jesus answers by pointing to the things taking place; the miracles and the evangel being proclaimed to the poor.

This seems to imply that the purpose of these manifestations is to say, "I am the One."

Since miracles accompany the teaching and preaching concerning the kingdom, it would seem that the purpose of these miracles is to proclaim in a way more powerful than words that the kingdom is near.

If this is true, and if Israel and the coming kingdom are now temporarily set aside (Romans 11:25) what can we infer about miracles in our present day?

Perhaps until God turns once again to Israel, this may not be the day for miracles.

++

Now let us pause to consider a very interesting comment Jesus makes about ...

Milestones in the Gospels (The Visitation)

> ### Trail Marker #8
> # Tyre, Sidon, and Sodom (11:21)

As for the cities who witness His powerful deeds but do not repent, woe unto them. If these acts had been witnessed in Tyre and Sidon long ago, they would have repented.

But why were Tyre and Sidon not given the same opportunity of witnessing miracles that might cause them to repent?

If the unrepentant in Tyre and Sidon are cast into an endless torment, this would not seem just.

But if ultimately every knee will bow and if all will be reconciled, then what appears to be an injustice against Tyre and Sidon may have actually served a purpose as God works progressively thru history toward the goal of reconciling all mankind unto Himself.

Jesus goes on ...

Likewise, it will be more tolerable for Sodom in the day of judging than for Capernaum. Capernaum will subside to the unseen.

Unseen is the Greek word *hades* and is translated *hell* in the KJV and *depths* in the NIV. If the people of Sodom will receive a lesser judgment than Capernaum, what will their judgment be? If both experience endless torment as some would teach, how is one receiving a lesser judgment than the other?

++

Chapter 12. The Pharisees make plans to kill Jesus.

And then, another stopping point ...

> Trail Marker #9
> # The unpardoned sin (12:22)

Therefore, every sin and blasphemy shall be pardoned men, yet the blasphemy of the spirit shall not be pardoned. And whoever may be saying a word against the Son of Mankind it will be pardoned him, yet whoever may be saying aught against the holy spirit it shall not be pardoned him, neither in this eon nor in that which is impending.

Much has been said, and many speculations made, concerning *the unpardoned sin* ("unpardonable" in some translations).

From the context we see that the offenders were guilty not because they opposed Jesus, but because they attributed the work of God to Satan. God's holy spirit was operating, but they claimed it was the power of Satan. Such rejection of God, or failure to recognize God, will not be forgiven in the present eon nor in the impending eon.

Eon (*aion* in the Greek) is often translated eternal, carrying the thought of endlessness. But observe here two different eons; the *present* eon and the *impending* eon.

Eon must, therefore, be a finite period of time with beginning and end. There is the present eon and another eon yet to come in the future.

And as for those committing *the unpardoned sin*, they will not be forgiven in this present eon or in the one to follow, but this does not mean forgiveness will not come after that. The unpardoned sin does not condemn a person "forever and ever."

++

Our next stopping point ...

> Trail Marker #10
> ## Parables – Locking the kingdom (13:1)

Jesus tells the throngs many things in parables, beginning with the parable of the sower. The disciples ask Jesus why He speaks in parables to the throngs. He answers, *To you has it been given to know the SECRETS of the kingdom of the heavens, yet to those it has not been given.*

Parables were not used to make truth easier to understand, but to reveal secrets to some while CONCEALING them from others.

At first the kingdom was proclaimed openly, but the Jewish leaders began rejecting it. Now Jesus proclaims in parables to conceal from most while revealing only to His closest followers; those to whom He has chosen to reveal.

Jesus explains, *Therefore in parables am I speaking to them, seeing that, observing, they are not observing, and hearing, they are not hearing, neither are they understanding. And filled up in them is the prophecy of Isaiah, that is saying, 'In hearing, you will be hearing, and may by no means be understanding, and observing, you will be observing, and may by no means be perceiving.' For stoutened is the heart of this people.* (13:13; Isaiah 6:9,10)

With these words it seems that the kingdom has been LOCKED to the majority, with explanations and revelation given only to the closest disciples. The quote from Isaiah shows the intent that the people will be hearing, but not understanding; for their hearts are *stoutened*. From this point on Jesus speaks to the throngs only in parables.

Remember that Jesus began by proclaiming the kingdom was NEAR, but now it appears to be LOCKED for the remainder of His ministry. Jumping ahead for a moment, Jesus will later tell the Jewish leaders, *You are <u>locking</u> the kingdom of the heavens in front of men. For you are not entering, neither are you letting those entering to enter* (Matthew 23:13).

Peter is given the keys; *I will be giving you the keys of the kingdom of the heavens,* (Matthew 16:19) and in Acts 2 we see Peter use the keys to "unlock" the kingdom, proclaiming it openly once again. But after repeated rejection, and especially after the the rejection by the Jewish leaders in the final chapter of Acts, the kingdom is locked once again. Paul uses the same words from Isaiah 6 that Jesus had used to lock the kingdom.

And today the Jews, and the kingdom's coming upon the earth, are delayed *until the complement of the nations may be entering.* (Romans 11:25) Paul's *evangel of the uncircumcision* (Galatians 2:7) is now the appropriate message until it is time once again for the *kingdom evangel* to be proclaimed; which will happen during the Tribulation period recorded by John in Revelation.

Milestones in the Gospels *(The Visitation)*

++ Some observations along the way ++

Continuing on ... more parables in chapter 13. And then Jesus returns to His own country.

But those knowing His family wonder how He could have wisdom or perform powerful deeds. Jesus observes, A prophet is not dishonored except in his own country and in his home. And He does <u>not</u> do many powerful deeds there *because of their unbelief.*

So it appears that <u>miracles</u> follow <u>belief</u> as the kingdom evangel is proclaimed, and where there is unbelief there will be no miracles.

Miracles were a *means* used by Jesus during the time He proclaimed the nearness of the kingdom. They would become less frequent as disbelief and rejection grew.

++

Jesus learns of John the Baptist's death and retires into the wilderness, privately.

He has compassion on the throngs and heals those who are ailing. He miraculously feeds 5000 who had followed Him into the wilderness. He walks on the water, displaying His authority over nature.

And at Gennesaret all who have an illness are brought to Him, and those who touch the tassel of His cloak are healed.

And then we encounter our next stopping point ...

Trail Marker #11
Tradition – the error of the Pharisees (15:1)

The scribes and Pharisees say the disciples are transgressing the *tradition* of the elders by not washing their hands before eating. Jesus responds that the scribes and Pharisees transgress *the precept of God*, and they *invalidate the word of God* because of their tradition.

The religious leaders had placed their own traditions above the word of God itself. The many rules they created and imposed upon the people were more important to them than what the word of God actually said.

Are the leaders within the church today guilty of the same, at least at times?

++

Our next stop ...

Trail Marker #12
Healing a gentile (15:22)

Jesus is approached by a Canaanite woman asking Him to heal her demonized daughter. Jesus points out that He was not commissioned *except for the lost sheep of Israel.* (15:24)

But the woman persists, worshipping Jesus. She reminds Jesus that even puppies eat the scraps falling from the master's table. Jesus replies, Great is your faith, and He heals the daughter.

Again we see that Jesus' commission is exclusively to the lost sheep of Israel. Here blessing had come to a Gentile, but only after initial resistance, for He had come for Israel. That was His commission.

Gentiles are only blessed indirectly, as in this case. Yet many Gentiles in the organized church today try to take all that Jesus said to Israel in the era of His earthly ministry and apply it directly to the church today.

This incident does not mark a new direction in Jesus' ministry. He will continue to go strictly to the sheep of Israel. Gentiles are only benefactors of His ministry indirectly; because of Israel. They receive, as this woman puts it, scraps from under Israel's table.

All Scripture is inspired by God, and is beneficial for teaching ...
(2 Timothy 3:16)

BUT ...

Endeavor to present yourself to God qualified, an unashamed worker, correctly cutting ["rightly dividing" in many translations] *the word of truth.* (2 Timothy 2:15)

Milestones in the Gospels *(The Visitation)*

> Trail Marker #13
>
> # Worship (15:25)

What can we learn from the Canaanite woman about WORSHIP?

The Greek word translated <u>worship</u> is *proskuneo*, which literally means "toward-teem."

Our notion of what worship consists of has been shaped by the religious traditions and ideas of men. To determine the true meaning of worship as used in the Scriptures we should examine every instance where the word is used. Using the Keyword Concordance which is contained within the Concordant Literal New Testament, we can study every occurrence of *proskuneo*.

We read that the Canaanite woman *coming, worships Him*. We learn from this instance that worship does not always occur within a group setting, and it is not always done thru singing as some today believe. If we examine every occurrence of the word in the New Testament we will see that worship is simply a coming near, a reverence for, and a faith in the object of worship; whatever outward shape this may take.

++ Some observations along the way ++

More healings ... the throngs marvel and glorify the God is <u>Israel</u> ... a miraculous feeding of 4000 ... and then once again Jesus warns His listeners to beware of the Pharisees.

And then a very important, and in my opinion one of the most misunderstood passages in the Scriptures ...

> Trail Marker #14
> ## Upon this rock (16:18)

You are Peter, and on this rock will I be building My ecclesia, and the gates of the unseen shall not be prevailing against it. I will be giving you the keys of the kingdom of the heavens.

On this rock could refer to Peter, or it could refer to Peter's *faith* that prompted his acknowledgement of Jesus being the Christ. The Greek word for Peter is *petros*, and the Greek for rock is *petra*.

But does this passage represent the beginning of "the Church?"

Most within the organized church today insist that this is the case as it is typically translated *upon this rock will I be building <u>my church</u>*. The Greek *ekklesia*, usually (though not always) translated *church*, simply means <u>called-out-ones</u> (*ek* – out; *klesia* – called).

If we examine *ekklesia* in every instance where it is found we will see that it does not always refer to the same group of called-out-ones in every case. It is used to refer to an assembly in Moses' day, (Acts 7:38) an unruly mob, (Acts 19:32) and a legal assembly like a jury. (Acts 19:39)

An ecclesia is simply a group of people *called out* from the general masses for a particular purpose.

Even in cases where ecclesia is a group that God has *called out*, can we assume it is always the same group (i.e. today's church)?

Those called out in Jesus' day and in the book of Acts were exclusively Jewish believers whose expectation was the kingdom from heaven to come upon the earth. But those called out in Paul's day are Jews and Gentiles alike called into one "body," whose expectation is in the heavenly realm. (1 Thessalonians 4:13)

Therefore when Jesus proclaims to Peter, *On this rock will I build My <u>called-out-ones</u>*, He speaks of the out-called Jews who are hearing the kingdom evangel and who are preparing for the kingdom to be established upon the earth, as it had been in David's day.

Trail Marker #15
The keys of the kingdom (16:19)

Are the KEYS of the kingdom related to the previous reference to the LOCKING of the kingdom?

When Jesus says to Peter, *I will be giving you the KEYS of the kingdom of the heavens,* this implies that the kingdom is "locked" and that keys are needed to open it. This concept is confirmed by the fact that Jesus has been talking about the kingdom only thru parables to conceal understanding from the masses.

When the holy spirit comes at Pentecost (Acts 2) we see the keys coming to Peter. Peter becomes the focal point and is given signs and wonders to accompany the kingdom proclamation, as had been the case when Jesus proclaimed the kingdom.

But as the kingdom continues to be rejected by the Jews in Acts, Peter fades and Paul takes the forefront. The keys given to Peter are no longer in use as Acts comes to an end. A new age had begun. Paul no longer proclaims the kingdom evangel to the Jews but instead the evangel of grace and reconciliation to the Gentiles.

Milestones in the Gospels *(The Visitation)*

++ Some observations along the way ++

Jesus predicts His death. He must come to Jerusalem where He will suffer and be killed, and on the third day roused.

Chapter 17. The transfiguration, witnessed by Peter, James, and John. Then another healing ... this time an epileptic boy. And Jesus again tells of His coming death.

Chapter 18. Jesus teaches that humility, like that of a little child, is needed to enter the kingdom. So His teaching continues to focus on the requirements for entry into the kingdom.

The parable of the lost sheep expresses the heart of the Father; to seek the one who is straying. The shepherd leaves the 99 to seek the one that has strayed.

Will God's heart change? Will He be satisfied to give up on the many who are led astray and who are tormented "endlessly" in a fiery hell? *It is not the will of your Father that one of these little ones should perish.*

Jesus tells Peter a brother should be pardoned *seventy times seven*. This should cause us to ask ... would a God who stresses the need for repeated forgiveness come to the point where He, Himself, will not forgive those being tormented "endlessly" in hell?

In the *parable of the unmerciful servant* we learn that pardon can be revoked. Because the slave whose debt had been forgiven refuses to forgive the debt of his fellow slave, the king revokes his forgiveness and requires payment of the debt.

This is the difference between pardon and justification. Pardon is something a king (executive) has the authority to grant. Justification, which Paul talks about, is something a judge (judicial) has the authority to grant. Pardon is taking one who is found guilty and suspending their sentence. Justification is finding someone innocent of the charges. There is a big difference.

When studying the Scriptures we must take care to observe things that are different and not mix them together. As we continue our studies let us observe the differences between such things as born again vs. new creation, kingdom of God vs. the celestial realm (heaven), and the evangel of the kingdom vs. the evangel of grace.

Chapter 19. Many more are healed. And Jesus talks about divorce. What God yokes together let not man be separating. God prohibits divorce in the law. But remember; the law cannot save. It can only show man his inabilities and imperfection.

So we must not, in the current age, use this passage to "enforce" the law pertaining to divorce. Still, we should recognize that God hates divorce, and the matter should not be taken lightly.

Jesus speaks more about entering the kingdom when speaking with the rich young man who asks what he should be doing to have life eonian. Jesus replies that if he wants to be <u>perfect</u> he should sell his possessions and give to the poor.

The question is posed, if it is easier for a camel to enter thru the eye of a needle than for a rich man to enter the kingdom of God, then who can be saved?

In other words, if it is up to man to meet the requirements of the Law, who can be saved? Jesus responds, *With men this is impossible, yet with God all is possible.*

++

Let us pause for a moment at this stopping point ...

> **Trail Marker #16**
>
> ## With men this is impossible, yet with God all is possible.
> (19:26)

So, Jesus takes the focus away from the efforts of men, which are insufficient. He places the focus upon the works of God, with Whom all things are possible.

The requirements to enter the kingdom which will be restored upon the earth seem impossible to keep. How can one exhibit *superabounding righteousness* (5:20) or *perfection* (5:48)? Now we read, *With men this is impossible, yet with God all is possible.*

Could it be that all we have read thus far has had the purpose of demonstrating to mankind that they are unable to meet the requirements to enter the kingdom, despite the best of intentions and effort?

Could God be progressively leading mankind (thus far only Israel) to the point where we understand it is only God's grace that can save us?

> ## Trail Marker #17
> ## Judging the 12 tribes of Israel
> ### (19:28)

Jesus speaks of the rewards for those who follow. When the Son of Man is seated on the throne they will *sit on twelve thrones, judging the twelve tribes of Israel.*

Again we see Jesus' ministry is directed to ISRAEL and not to those of the nations. The kingdom, when restored upon the earth, will see Israel serving as God's instrument to accomplish His will, and the Twelve will reign with Him.

This is fulfilled in Revelation. Throughout Revelation we will see a very Jewish character. Paul's "joint heirs" is not referred to, but instead we will see the kingdom with preference given to the Jews.

This makes sense. The kingdom that was being introduced by Jesus, and later by Peter, is postponed when the Jews continually reject the kingdom message. When the kingdom agenda is temporarily set aside, Paul introduces a new thing; the Body of Christ comprised of Gentile and Jew alike with neither having superiority. (Ephesians 2:11)

But in the end times which we see in Revelation, the kingdom agenda returns as God completes His work within the ages. In the final eon we see the righteous Jews upon the earth with Christ reigning upon the throne. The Body of Christ is serving in the heavenly realms, not upon the earth. (Ephesians 2:6, 2 Timothy 2:12, 4:18, 1 Corinthians 6:3)

Milestones in the Gospels *(The Visitation)*

++ Some observations along the way ++

Chapter 20. Another parable; then Jesus again predicts His death. And another healing as He leaves Jericho; restoring sight to two blind men.

Chapter 21. The triumphal entry into Jerusalem. Money changers are expelled from the Temple.

And a fig tree withers at a word spoken by Jesus. The fig tree appears to be symbolic of Israel as a nation. They were called to be baptized and to bear fruit. Instead they rejected their king repeatedly. Now, near the end of Jesus' life and ministry, He symbolically curses the fig tree (Israel). No fruit would come from Israel in the present eon.

Israel will again hear the proclamation concerning the kingdom in Acts, following the crucifixion and resurrection of Christ, but there would be no fruit. The stage is being set for the temporary setting aside of Israel as God's grace is extended to the nations (as Paul describes in Romans 11:25).

More parables. The parable of the two sons and the vineyard, and the parable of the wicked vinedressers both speak of the kingdom. In the latter Jesus asks, *Did you never read in the scriptures, the stone that was rejected by the builders came to be the head of the corner? The kingdom of God will be taken from you and given to a nation producing its fruits.*

This prophesies the setting aside of Israel, with the evangel going to the Gentile nations thru Paul. But the kingdom is not *permanently* taken from Israel as we see from Paul's words. (Romans 11:25) The kingdom that is eventually restored upon the earth in Revelation is clearly Jewish in character.

Chapter 22. Another parable ... the wedding banquet. The Pharisees consult to trap Jesus. And in Chapter 23, Jesus proclaims another warning concerning the scribes and Pharisees.

Woe to the scribes and Pharisees, for they are hypocrites. They are LOCKING the kingdom of the heavens in front of men; not entering nor letting those entering to enter.

Jesus laments over Jerusalem.

Trail Marker #18
The Olivet Discourse (24:3)

Chapter 24. Jesus predicts the destruction of the temple. And when the disciples ask what will be the sign of His presence and the conclusion of the eon, He replies with what is commonly called "The Olivet Discourse."

Jesus warns them not to be deceived, for many will come saying they are the Christ. They will hear of battles, nation will be roused against nation and kingdom against kingdom, there will be famines and quakes; and these are just the beginning of the pangs.

Followers will be given up and afflicted. Many will be snared and will be giving one another up.

There will be many false prophets who will deceive many, and there will be a growing lawlessness. The love of many will be cooling.

He who endures to the consummation shall be saved.

The evangel of the kingdom will be heralded to the whole earth as a testimony to all the nations, and *then the consummation will be arriving.*

Jesus appears to be referring to the fulfillment of what is commonly called The Great Commission. (28:16) Note from Jesus' words that this is not something that appears to be imminent in His day, but will occur just prior to His return to the earth.

These events will occur before the end of the age (the *consummation*) but will be preceded by battles, famines, false prophets, etc. During the end times (of which we read in Revelation) Israel will serve as God's instrument upon the earth, proclaiming the kingdom evangel as a testimony to all nations.

But today, in our current era, it is not appropriate to proclaim the *evangel of the kingdom*.

Yes, this evangel was announced by Jesus, and even later (in Acts) by Peter; but always to ISRAEL. Today the kingdom has been temporarily set aside (Romans 11:25-6) and we within the Body of Christ are to proclaim the evangel God has revealed for this age; the *evangel of the uncircumcision*; the evangel of grace.

We have absolutely no authority or commission to proclaim the evangel of the kingdom or the "Great Commission" today.

Jesus proceeds with some details concerning the end time events commonly known as the Great Tribulation (24:15).

When the abomination of desolation as declared through Daniel the prophet is standing in the holy place (Daniel 11:31; 12:11) they are to flee. There will be a great affliction unlike any that occurred before, and unless the days are discounted no flesh at all would be saved. But because of the chosen the days will be discounted.

If anyone says they are the Christ, they are not to be believed. The coming of the true Christ will be as lightning from east to west (i.e. clearly observed).

So the return of Christ will be clearly evident; as lightning from east to west. History records no such event. Christ's return is still an event to be anticipated.

But false christs and false prophets will use great signs and miracles to deceive. After the sun and moon are darkened and the stars fall and the powers of the heavens are shaken, then will appear the sign of the Son of Man in heaven. All the *tribes* shall grieve.

Tribes refer to Israel, often referred to as the twelve tribes, who have opposed Christ. They will see the Son of Man coming on the clouds, (24:30) dispatching His messengers with a loud trumpet, and His chosen from the extremities of the earth will be assembled. The true coming of the Son of Man should not be confused with the claims of the false christs or false prophets.

++ Some observations along the way ++

The parable of the fig tree, the parable of the faithful and evil servants, and the parable of the wise and foolish virgins emphasize the need to be watchful.

Milestones in the Gospels *(The Visitation)*

> ### Trail Marker #19
> # No one knows the day or hour
> (24:34)

By no means may this generation be passing by till all these things should be occurring.

This seems to indicate that the end would occur during the lifetime of those hearing Jesus speak. But note that these things *should* be occurring in their lifetime, yet because of Israel's hardness they did *not* occur at that time.

Jesus did not reveal the "pause" that would occur as Israel continued to reject the coming kingdom during the period described in Acts. In Acts and then Paul's letters we will see that because the kingdom is rejected despite many proclamations, Israel will be temporarily set aside until the full complement of the nations may enter. (Romans 11:25-6)

Despite the signs that will occur (e.g. the fig tree), <u>no one knows the day or hour</u> when the Son of Man will come; not the messengers, nor the Son; but only the Father. The coming of the Son of Man will be as the days of Noah, where there was eating, drinking and marrying until Noah entered the ark. They did not know when the deluge was coming until it came.

It is interesting that despite these clear instructions there have been many through the years that have been able to deceive by predicting the exact time of Christ's return, often citing Biblical evidence to substantiate their claims.

Be watching for you are not aware on what day your Lord is coming. (24:42)
In an hour you are not supposing, the Son of Man is coming. (24:44)

++ Some observations along the way ++

Chapter 25. The parable of the talents reminds Jesus' audience (Israel) to be good and faithful stewards until He returns.

And then we come to a well-known passage …

> **Trail Marker #20**
> # The sheep & the goats (25:31)

The *parable of the sheep and goats* foretells the return of Christ. When the Son of Mankind comes in His glory He will be seated on the throne. All nations will be gathered before Him and He will sever the sheep from the kids.

The sheep will enjoy the allotment of the kingdom. *As you do it to one of the least of My brethren, you do it to Me.* These (the *just*) come away into life eonian.

The goats will be sent away cursed into the fire eonian made ready for the Adversary and his messengers. *As you do it not to one of the least, you do it not to Me.* These shall come away into chastening eonian.

Note that this judgment is based on works, not faith.

And no indication is given that this refers to the resurrection. The nations that are upon the earth are gathered by the Son of Man for judgment and they are judged based on how they treated God's chosen people (Israel).

The reward (life) and the penalty (chastening) are not endless, but *eonian*.

And the word here translated *chastening* is the Greek *kolasis* and it means in all instances a chastening for the good of the subject, as a tree is pruned for the good of the tree. How can it be for the good of the subject if the chastening goes on endlessly?

Furthermore, if we examine all instances where the Greek word *aion* is used it is clear that it cannot possibly convey the idea of endlessness.

Milestones in the Gospels *(The Visitation)*

++ Some observations along the way ++

Chapter 26 records the last week of Christ's visitation upon the earth. He foretells His coming crucifixion to the disciples, as the chief priests and elders meet with Caiaphas, the Chief Priest, to plot against Jesus.

Jesus is anointed, and He shares the Passover meal with His disciples. He goes to Gethsemane where he prays while the disciples sleep. Judas leads a throng to Jesus and He is arrested. Peter denies Him.

Chapter 27. After a brief trial He is led away to be crucified. After His death He is buried by Joseph of Arimathea, a rich man and a disciple of Jesus, in his new tomb with a large stone at the door. Remembering that Jesus said He would be roused after three days, Pilate assigns a detail to secure the tomb.

Chapter 28. At the lighting up into *one of the sabbaths*, Mary Magdalene and the other Mary come to the sepulcher.

> ## Trail Marker #21
> ## One of the sabbaths (28:1)

One of the Sabbaths is often erroneously translated the *first day of the week*, giving the notion that the resurrection occurred on Sunday. There is no linguistic warrant to render the translation in this way; it is only carelessness and the contamination of the Scriptures by religious tradition. There is no word in the Greek for first, or day, or week found anywhere in this passage.

The problem is the thinking that *Sabbath* always refers to the weekly Sabbath (Saturday), but Leviticus 23 summarizes seven festivals or feasts that are referred to as *special Sabbaths*.

Some Sabbaths occur in close proximity. For example, on the tenth day of the seventh month we have the Day of Covering (Atonement) and five days later is another Sabbath; the Festival of Ingathering.

The *evening of the Sabbaths* is where an evening ends one Sabbath and begins another. Occasionally a festival falls on the weekly Sabbath, in which case we have a double Sabbath, or *the day of the Sabbaths*.

When we see the phrase *one of the Sabbaths* it refers to the series of Sabbaths between Wave Sheaf and Pentecost. In 28:1 we have just concluded Passover a few days earlier, and *one of the Sabbaths* would refer to the regular weekly Sabbath; a Saturday.

++ Some observations along the way ++

A great quake occurs. A messenger of the Lord from heaven rolls away the stone. From fear the keepers quake and become as the dead.

A messenger says to the women, He is not here; He was roused. Go, tell His disciples that He was roused from the dead. He is preceding you into Galilee; there you will see Him.

As they go, Jesus meets them. They hold His feet and worship Him. Jesus instructs them, Fear not! Go, tell My brethren to come into Galilee, and there they shall see Me.

Trail Marker #22
The Great Commission (28:16)

The eleven disciples go into Galilee, to the mountain where Jesus arranged with them. Jesus tells them,

Given to Me was all authority in heaven and on the earth. Going, then, disciple all the nations, baptizing them into the name of the Father, Son and holy spirit ... teaching them to be keeping all, whatever I direct you. I am with you all the days till the conclusion of the eon!

The Greek verb distinguishes between completeness and incompleteness rather than time. *Given to Me was all* authority (28:18) appears to be in the past tense, but this statement is not yet realized. This will be fulfilled when the seventh trumpet sounds (Revelation 11:15). There we read, *The kingdom of this world became our Lord's and His Christ's, and He shall be reigning for the eons of the eons.*

But why didn't the disciples carry out "the great commission" after the resurrection of Christ?

If the disciples thought "The Great Commission" was to be carried out immediately why did they not act accordingly? They did not go to the nations at any time during their ministries.

Could it be that they understood it was not yet time to *disciple all the nations* but that this would occur later, as we see in Revelation?

This would be consistent with Jesus' description of the end times when He says, *Heralded shall be this evangel of the kingdom in the whole inhabited earth for a testimony to all the nations, and* <u>then</u> *the consummation shall be arriving.* (24:14)

Now we proceed to Mark's gospel account ...

Mark

Mark's account covers many of the same events as Matthew but from a different perspective, for Mark has a different purpose.

Matthew portrayed Jesus as CHRIST *(Messiah)* and KING. For this reason we saw the extensive genealogy to prove that Jesus was qualified. And there were many references from Old Testament prophecy to show that Jesus fulfilled these prophecies.

But Mark portrays Jesus as a SERVANT; the SON OF MAN. There is no genealogy, as none is needed for his purpose.

We must remember that the four gospel accounts are not simply four duplicate narratives of the life of Jesus. They were not intended to be "harmonized" as many attempt to do. Each writer has a specific and singular purpose that determined his selection and arrangement of material.

Matthew portrays Jesus as *King,*
Mark as *Servant,*
Luke as *Man,* and
John as *Son of God.*

++

As we proceed thru the remaining three gospel accounts we will not repeat our observations on similar events. We will simply stop along the way at some new points of interest.

Our first stopping point in Mark ...

> Trail Marker #23
> ## The purpose of His ministry (1:38)

When the disciples find Jesus and report that all are seeking Him, Jesus replies, *We may be going elsewhere, into the next towns, that there also I should be <u>heralding</u> ... for <u>for this I came out</u>.*

Notice that His ministry is not for the purpose of healing or casting out demons but to HERALD His message.

This primary mission is *accompanied* by healing and the casting out of demons. Miracles will validate His identity and authority, but <u>His purpose is to herald</u> the message He is commissioned to proclaim.

And remember that His message concerns *the evangel of the kingdom of God.* (1:14) The kingdom is *near*.

Think back to the days of David and Solomon when the kingdom established by God was at its peak. But then came division and rebellion and exile. The prophets promised restoration of the kingdom and a return to the land. This is the expectation of Israel.

Now comes the Son of God (Jesus) to prepare the sheep of Israel to enter the kingdom when it is restored. It is <u>near</u>, and His evangel is intended to <u>prepare</u> Israel.

Repentance and belief are closely tied to the message. Will Israel believe as He heralds this good news? Will they repent and prepare themselves to enter the coming kingdom?

> **Trail Marker #24**
> # Tradition (7:1)

Pharisees and scribes come from Jerusalem and ask why Jesus' disciples are not walking in accord with the tradition of the elders, as they do not wash their hands before eating.

But the Pharisees and scribes had repudiated the precepts of God while holding the tradition of men. They *invalidate* the word of God by their tradition.

Observe this lesson concerning the precepts of God as contrasted with the traditions of men, and consider the contrast between the precepts of God and the religious rules and teachings within the organized churches of our day.

How many things are taught in churches today as being precepts of God, when in fact they are traditions of men? Drinking? Smoking? Baptism requirements? Sabbath keeping for the Body of Christ? Church-going?

Are these based on a correct, "rightly divided" (2 Timothy 2:15) interpretation of the Scriptures, or man-made traditions?

Trail Marker #25
Destroying one's soul (8:34)

If anyone is wanting to come after Me, let him renounce himself and pick up his cross and follow Me. For whosoever may be wanting to save his soul will be destroying it, yet whoever shall be destroying his soul on account of Me and of the evangel will be saving it. For what is it benefiting a man to gain the whole world and forfeit his soul?

The *soul* is the consciousness aspect of life. The soul was generated when God took mere soil and animated it with His spirit.

Joining the spirit and soil to create the soul (consciousness/life) might be compared with applying electricity to a filament to produce light.

To gain the world (worldly gain) and forfeit the soul (conscious life) refers to forfeiting life in the eon/age to come when Christ restores the kingdom upon the earth.

But this does not mean the offender will forfeit life at a future time when all is restored at the end of the eons as described in 1 Corinthians 15 when God becomes All in all.

Milestones in the Gospels *(The Visitation)*

> Trail Marker #26
> # Prayer (11:22)

If you have faith of God, verily, I am saying to you that whosoever may be saying to this mountain, Be picked up and cast into the sea, and may not be doubting in his heart, but should be believing that what he is speaking is occurring, it shall be his, whatsoever he may be saying.

Therefore I am saying to you, All, whatever you are praying and requesting, be believing that you obtained, and it will be yours.

These instructions for faith and prayer are not a blank check for all peoples in all ages ... that whatever is asked for will be received as long as there is unwavering faith.

Jesus was speaking TO THE TWELVE. And these remarks are related to the coming kingdom; a kingdom that will physically come upon the earth, where earthly healings, signs and wonders were a part of the evangel being proclaimed.

But later, in Paul's ministry, when Israel is temporarily set aside and when Paul shares the evangel intended for the Body of Christ, grace is sufficient.

Within the Body of Christ our expectation is not the kingdom to come upon the earth. We await our Lord's call to join Him in the heavens where we will serve Him.

Logically, earth-bound signs and wonders do not relate to the evangel intended for the Body of Christ in our present era. Our expectation is not upon this earth as was the case with Israel.

Luke

> Trail Marker #27
>
> ## Whosoever the Son may be intending to unveil Him (10:22)

All was given up to Me by My Father, and no one knows who the Son is except the Father, and who the Father is except the Son, and <u>whomsoever the Son may be intending to unveil Him</u>.

It is not a matter of being more intelligent or commendable in recognizing and accepting the Lord and the kingdom. Those who understand and receive Him are those to whom He unveils Himself.

But why does He not simply unveil Himself to all? Could it be that those who reject Him in these days are playing a necessary part in God's plan to ultimately save all?

Consider Joseph's brothers who meant their deeds to harm Joseph, when in fact all that happened to Joseph was God's intent in order to carry out His ultimate plan?

> Trail Marker #28
> ## The Rich Man & Lazarus (16:19)

A poor man (Lazarus) and a rich man both die. The rich man, in torment, sees Abraham from afar and Lazarus with him. He asks Abraham to be merciful to him, but is reminded that he received his good things in his lifetime while Lazarus received evil things.

The rich man is not able to cross the great chasm between them. He asks that at least Lazarus be sent to warn his brothers so they do not also come to *this place of torment*, but Abraham replies: If they do not hear Moses and the prophets, neither will they be persuaded if someone should rise from among the dead.

This account is found only in Luke. Confusion and misunderstanding occur when one attempts to literalize a portion of Scripture that is figurative. The story of the rich man and Lazarus is clearly a figurative teaching about stewardship that started in 15:1 with the parables of the lost sheep, the lost coin and the prodigal son.

Some try to use this portion of Scripture as proof of the state of wicked sinners after death. They are conscious, engulfed in flames and in extreme torment for all eternity. But let's make a few observations.

1. Some say the rich man and Lazarus is not a parable because Jesus did not specifically identify it as a parable. But Jesus also did not say that the stories of the lost coin, the prodigal or the unjust steward are parables; yet most will agree they are. Consider the context. The rich man is one more in a series of parables in Luke 15-16.

2. Many teachers in the day who spoke in Semitic environments often used symbolism and parables. Often incidents are greatly exaggerated to amplify the teaching. Consider the mustard seed which does not literally grow into the largest of trees. (Matthew 13:32) And when Paul suggests one heap coals of fire onto the head of one's enemy, was this to be taken literally? (Romans 12:20)

3. Jesus Himself reached the point in His ministry that when talking with the masses He spoke only in parables. (Matthew 13:34-35)

4. Lazarus ate crumbs that fell from the rich man's table. If this is to be taken literally, would Lazarus have eaten enough to survive?
5. When Lazarus went to reside in Abraham's bosom; the breast portion of his body ... is this to be taken literally?
6. If there was a large chasm between Abraham/Lazarus and the rich man, how were they able to talk with one another?
7. If Abraham and Lazarus are in heaven (as many claim), the redeemed would be in constant contact with the sinners being tormented in hell. Seeing the tortured persons writhing in pain, close enough to converse, how can the redeemed find enjoyment in their eternal state? One's unredeemed father, mother, spouse, child would also be suffering in plain view.
8. Does the rich man ask Lazarus to drag him out of the fire? No; but only to place a drop of cold water on his tongue. This would not relieve his pain in the slightest, so what is the point?
9. Who is the rich man? If the story is taken at face value, and if one believes it teaches things concerning one's eternal destiny in heaven or hell, consider this. Salvation would have nothing to do with faith or righteousness. Nothing is said of the rich man's character. He is not said to be wicked, dishonest, unjust or immoral. He is simply rich. Nor do we learn much of Lazarus. He is poor, but we are not told that he is righteous or good. Therefore one's eternal destiny, if this is what the story is about, is dependent upon being rich and enjoying the present life, or being poor and not enjoying the present life.
10. This is not simply any rich man. He calls Abraham his father. He is a legal possessor of Abraham's inheritance. He enjoyed the physical blessings given to Abraham's seed. He wore purple. Why would Jesus bother to say anything about the rich man's clothes? Purple is the symbol of kingship; and linen, the symbol of priesthood. In this story the rich man, representative of Israel, is unfaithful with his responsibilities.
11. The great chasm would seem to be similar to that which prevented Moses from entering the promised land, because of his rebellion. Likewise the rebellious of Israel will fail to enter the kingdom when it is established upon the earth.

12. Those charged with being stewards (the leaders of Israel) are not faithful, and their inheritance is forfeited. Those despised by the leaders of Israel (tribute collectors and sinners) are given the inheritance in their place.

13. For any that would use this parable to derive the idea that the dead are alive in a conscious state, this would be in direct contradiction to many other passages that clearly teach the dead know nothing and are in an unconscious sleep state, awaiting the resurrection. (Ecclesiastes 9:5)

14. For any who would believe the rich man and Lazarus is a teaching concerning heaven and hell, consider that Moses never taught anything about going to either heaven or hell. God only promises thru Moses good and bad things here on earth, which is why Israel's expectation was for a Messiah to come and free them from bondage. The Old Testament says nothing at all about one's reward being in heaven, or one's punishment being to burn in hell.

> Trail Marker #29
> ## Today ... in Paradise (23:43)

One of the malefactors on the cross beside Jesus says to Him, *Be reminded of me, Lord, whenever Thou mayest be coming in Thy kingdom. Verily, to you am I saying today, with Me shall you be in paradise.*

The original Greek manuscripts contained no punctuation. Punctuation in our English translations is interpretation.

Most versions render this passage: *I am saying, today you will be with me in paradise.* This supports the prevailing opinion that the one who dies goes immediately to heaven or hell.

But since the Scriptures in many passages tell us that there is no consciousness in the death state, at least until the resurrection, we see that the punctuation should be placed as follows: *I am saying today, you will be with me in paradise.*

John

> ## Trail Marker #30
> ## You must be born again (3:3)

Jesus says to Nicodemus, a Pharisee and a chief of the Jews, *If anyone should not be begotten of water and of spirit, he cannot be entering into the kingdom of God. ... You must be begotten anew.*

You (plural) must be *begotten anew*, or "born again."

Jesus is speaking not of Nicodemus as an individual, but ISRAEL. Israel is anticipating the Messiah and the restoration of the kingdom, and must be "born again" to enter it.

This passage is not directed to the Body of Christ or to the world at large. It is directed to ISRAEL. Israel must be "born again" to be ready for the kingdom that is to be restored upon the earth.

The Body of Christ is not commanded to be born again; we are a *new creation*. (2 Corinthians 5:17; Galatians 6:15) We are not told we must BECOME a new creation; we are MADE TO BE a new creation. It is all God, not human effort.

> **Trail Marker #31**
> # Indignation or life eonian (3:15)

He who believes in the Son has *life eonian*, but he who is stubborn as to the Son shall not be seeing life but *the indignation of God is REMAINING on him.*

Take note of a very key word; REMAINING.

All men apart from God are found wanting and God's indignation is on them. We will see this indignation in active form in Revelation.

But for now God introduces a solution; His only-begotten Son. Those who believe will have life in the kingdom upon the earth in the eons to come, but for those who are stubborn and who do not believe God's indignation REMAINS on them and they will not enjoy life within the kingdom when it is restored.

Later God will introduce a more "global" solution; once Israel's stubbornness causes her to be temporarily set aside (Romans 11:25) and reconciliation is offered to men of ALL nations without preference to Israel. Then God will require faith alone, and not faith PLUS obedience (works) as is the case when John records his account.

But in the era of Jesus' visitation upon the earth, God is speaking to ISRAEL in preparation for the kingdom's restoration upon the earth.

> Trail Marker #32
> ## Salvation is of the Jews (4:22)

Salvation is of the Jews. But coming is the hour, and now is, where the true worshipers will be worshiping the Father in spirit and truth. God is spirit, and those worshiping Him must worship in spirit and truth.

SALVATION IS OF THE JEWS! Salvation is extended to the nations, but only through Israel; until Paul later introduces a new revelation from God ... Israel and the nations as joint-heirs with no preference or distinction.

> ## Trail Marker #33
> ## None can come unless drawn (6:44)

No one can come to Me if ever the Father Who sends Me should not be DRAWING him.

Think about this! None are righteous. None are seeking God. (Romans 3:10-12) If the Father did not DRAW men to Himself, none could come. Christ is His means of doing this, and He begins with Israel.

No amount of human will and determination can cause one to believe in Christ if it is not given by the Father. The Father desires that ALL men be saved (1 Timothy 2:4) but His plan is to draw (not force; but *draw*) all men thru a progression of events.

All that we see in the Scriptures and in our world today is a work in progress that is leading to the point when God's will is finally accomplished, and He becomes All in all. (1 Corinthians 15:22-28)

During the time of Jesus' earthly visitation it is ISRAEL that plays a part in God's unfolding plan, and even among Israel some are given to believe while others *cannot* believe.

> ### Trail Marker #34
> ### They could not believe (12:37)

But after having done so many signs before them, they did not believe in Him. THEY COULD NOT BELIEVE, seeing that Isaiah said *He has blinded their eyes and callouses their heart, lest they may be perceiving with their eyes, and should be apprehending with their heart, and may be turning about.* [from Isaiah 6:9,10]

And so again we see that BELIEF is not something that one can simply develop through perseverance and effort. It is clearly stated here that some COULD NOT BELIEVE as their eyes had been blinded.

As God's progressive plan unfolds, some will believe and give testimony to others; while others CANNOT believe. But all is a work in progress leading to the point when one day ALL will believe and will be reconciled to God, for this is His desire and plan. (1 Timothy 2:4; Ephesians 1:11)

> ## Trail Marker #35
> ## Fear of the religious leaders (12:42)

Many of the chiefs *did* believe in Him, but because of the Pharisees they did not avow it for they would have been put out of the synagogue. They love the glory of men rather than the glory of God.

It is interesting that many in the church today are locked within the mindset of their church leaders. If truth is found in the Scriptures that is outside the bounds of the teachings of one's church they risk being *put out* of the church if they speak out.

This is especially true of church leaders and those leading Christian organizations, universities, etc. They are often locked in error because they wish not to be *put out* by questioning the creeds or statements of faith particular to their brand of Christianity. Often it is because *they love the glory of men rather than the glory of God.*

I was once told that creeds and orthodoxy protect the truth from heresy. I have come to find that creeds and orthodoxy lock men into error that has been espoused and preserved by the traditions of men.

Also notice the word synagogues. Clearly this speaks of believers within Israel.

> ## Trail Marker #36
> ## I came not to judge (12:47)

If any should be hearing My declarations and not be maintaining them, I am not judging him, for I came not that I should be judging the world, but that I should be saving the world.

He who is repudiating Me and not getting My declarations has that which is judging him. The word that I speak will be judging him in the last day, seeing that I speak not from Myself, but the Father Who sends Me.

There will come a day of judging. But that too will be a part of God's progressive plan, leading toward the ultimate reconciliation of ALL.

1. None are righteous.

2. None are even seeking God.

[So God's judgment would be upon ALL.]

3. Jesus comes; the Son of God and commissioned by God.

4. God enables SOME to believe and give testimony.

5. Judgment remains upon those not believing, but with the ultimate goal of leading to belief ... because it is God's will that ALL men are saved ... and He is working ALL in accord with the counsel of His will.

> **Trail Marker #37**
> ## Taught by the holy spirit (14:26)

The consoler, the holy spirit which the Father will be sending in My name, will be *teaching* you all and *reminding* you of all that I said to you.

This is Jesus talking with His disciples at this particular time. His disciples will be taught directly by the holy spirit, and those things will then be recorded in the Scriptures and preserved for later generations.

It is the Scriptures that provide us with God's teachings today, not supernatural teachings given directly by the holy spirit. That was a different era. Later we will read that Paul completed the word of God, (Colossians 1:25) and it is to the Word of God we must turn for teachings in our present era.

> Trail Marker #38
> # Doubting Thomas (20:24)

Thomas had not been with them when Jesus appeared. The other disciples tell him, We have seen the Lord ... but Thomas will not believe "should I not perceive in His hands the print of the nails, and thrust my hand into His side."

Eight days later Jesus appears again and says to Thomas, See My hands, and thrust your hand into My side. Thomas replies, My Lord and My God.

Seeing that you have seen Me, you have believed. Happy are those who are not seeing and believe.

Thomas is an example of those who do not believe by faith. Are they to be discarded and sent to an eternity of torment?

Thomas would not believe UNTIL he saw for himself. He was not rejected for his failure to believe by faith.

True, it is preferred that we believe by faith. *Happy are those who are not seeing and believe.* But those who do not ... who CANNOT believe ... will one day see the Lord face to face.

And they, like Thomas, will then believe. Will they be rejected for their failure to believe by faith in their lifetime when they had ample opportunity? Look to Thomas for the answer to that question.

++

As for the purpose of Christ Jesus' earthly ministry, Paul tells us: *Jesus Christ was a minister of the Circumcision for the truth of God, to confirm the promises made to the fathers.* (Romans 15:8).

Milestones as they Awaited the King's Return
"The Waiting"

An Overview of the Scriptures, by
BOB EVELY © *2018.*
An Independent Minister of Christ Jesus,
Of the church at Wilmore, Kentucky

The four "Gospels" (Matthew, Mark, Luke, John) give an account of the time when Jesus walked upon the earth. In those accounts we see Jesus (the king) proclaiming that the kingdom is near; referring to the restoration of the kingdom unto Israel. His audience was Israel!

But Israel would not receive her king. Jesus is crucified; and the kingdom is rejected. As Acts begins will the good news go now to the Gentiles instead of the Jews?

A close study of Acts is key in understanding the difference between the *expectation* and the *message* proclaimed to Israel, and the *expectation* and the *message* later proclaimed to the Body of Christ. By *expectation* I mean; what was the audience expecting or looking for in their future as they heard the message proclaimed?

Let us continue our journey, stopping at trail markers along the way to contemplate some key points.

Acts (Part 1)

Milestones as they Awaited the King's Return (The Waiting)

> ### Trail Marker #1
> ## When will the kingdom be restored? (1:6)

The apostles ask, Art thou at this time restoring the kingdom to Israel? Jesus replies, *Not yours is it to know times or eras which the Father placed in His own jurisdiction.*

Observe that Jesus does not tell them the kingdom will NOT be restored TO ISRAEL, but that it is not theirs to know the timing. We can infer, then, that the kingdom will indeed be restored *to Israel*; and we will see this occur when Christ returns in Revelation. But the TIME for this to happen is not yet revealed.

Remember that the prophets had foretold the coming Day of the Lord, when the Messiah would return to judge the world. This is the kingdom that is to come upon the earth. It was rejected by the Jews when Christ was crucified, but it is still anticipated at some future point.

++ Some observations along the way ++

Jesus tells them when the holy spirit comes on them and empowers them, they will be His witnesses.

He ascends from mount Olivet as two men tell those gathered that He will return in the same manner.

They return to Jerusalem. And as they wait, Judas is replaced by Matthias.

Milestones as they Awaited the King's Return *(The Waiting)*

> Trail Marker #2
> # Matthias replaces Judas (1:12)

What is the requirement for Judas' replacement? One who was *with us in all the time in which the Lord Jesus came in and out to us, beginning from the baptism of John until the day on which He was taken up from us.*

The mission for the apostles is *to become a witness of His resurrection.* (1:22)

Observe the importance of keeping the number of apostles at twelve!

The mission of the Twelve is to go to the tribes of Israel, just as Jesus had done throughout His lifetime. Jesus was not commissioned to go to all nations, but only to Israel. That was His commission.

It is interesting to note that there were twelve tribes in Israel, and twelve apostles commissioned to go to Israel. It is also interesting that later, when Paul becomes an apostle, he is <u>in addition to the Twelve</u>. He is never one of the Twelve!

This makes sense as Paul's mission was different ... to go to the Gentiles. Paul will become an apostle of a different kind, with a different assignment.

++ Some observations along the way ++

Chapter 2. Pentecost! ISRAELITES from all nations assemble in Jerusalem. They are *filled with holy spirit, and begin to speak in different languages, according as the spirit gave them to declaim.*

Many teach that the church was born at Pentecost. But we must remember that Pentecost was a Jewish feast, and the ecclesia ("church") we read about in Acts 2 consists exclusively of Jews.

Peter addresses those assembled.

Milestones as they Awaited the King's Return (The Waiting)

> Trail Marker #3
> ## Peter's address to the house of Israel (2:22)

Let all <u>the house of Israel</u> know that God makes Him Lord as well as Christ, this Jesus Whom you crucify.

Although Jesus, the Christ and King, has been rejected by the Jews and crucified, even at this point the evangel being proclaimed by the apostles is still going only to the house of Israel. (2:36)

When asked what they should we be doing, Peter responds, *Repent and be baptized each of you in the name of Jesus Christ, for the pardon of your sins, and you shall be obtaining the gratuity of the holy spirit. To you is the promise, and to your children, and to all those afar, whosoever the Lord our God should be calling to Him. Be saved from this crooked generation.*

At this point it is still the "kingdom evangel" that is being proclaimed to Israel, just as Jesus had proclaimed it. *Repent ... the kingdom is near.* The restoration of the kingdom unto Israel, upon the earth, is still anticipated and still lies ahead. The call is to repent.

And when the king returns, and when the kingdom is restored unto Israel, there will come the time of judging.

So at this point Peter is proclaiming that now is the time to repent and prepare for the king Who will come and judge. *Repent and be saved from His wrath and judgment.*

++ Some observations along the way ++

After the events of Pentecost there were about 3000 souls added to the ecclesia, and *the Lord was adding to those being saved daily*. The ecclesia persevered in the teaching of the apostles, fellowship, breaking bread, and prayer.

Many MIRACLES and SIGNS occur thru the apostles in Jerusalem.

They were all in the same place and had all things in common; dividing possessions as some would have need.

Milestones as they Awaited the King's Return (The Waiting)

> Trail Marker #4
>
> # The Ecclesia [2]

The *ecclesia* (commonly translated "church" in most versions) consisted only of Israelites at this point. They met in the sanctuary. Consider Acts 21:28 where the Jews become enraged when they think Paul had taken a Gentile into the sanctuary.

Take care when attempting to apply things we are reading thus far in Acts to our present age. The *gospel* at this time is going out only to Israel, and the *ecclesia* (church) consists only of Israelites.

Ecclesia simply means *out-called ones*, or those who have been *called out* from the whole of mankind for some particular purpose. Ecclesia does not always mean the same thing in every context, and most modern Bible translations confuse things by using the word church; causing us to think that all instances are talking directly to or about the church as we know it today.

As we read on we must remember that at this point in Acts the *ecclesia* is comprised only of Israelites. They are the ones *called out* by God at this point.

> **Trail Marker #5**
> # Signs & Wonders (3)

Chapter 3. Peter heals a lame man.

In Jesus' earthly ministry signs and wonders closely accompanied the proclaiming of the kingdom evangel. We see this continuing in the time of the apostles; the *Pentecostal administration*. This is how God was operating as the kingdom evangel was being proclaimed to Israel.

But can we assume that God *must* be operating in the same way today?

Israel was promised earthly blessings ... land, physical blessings and curses based on obedience, and the restoration of the kingdom upon the earth. Does it not make sense that the proclamation of these things to Israel would be accompanied by physical signs and wonders upon this earth?

But is the expectation for the Body of Christ in this present age the same?

No; we have been promised spiritual blessings, and our expectation is not for the kingdom to be restored upon this earth, but for a celestial kingdom; and for Christ to call us upward to meet Him in the air where we will serve Him in the celestial realm. (1 Thessalonians 4:13ff)

With *spiritual* promises and expectations can we rightly assume we will be given *earthly* signs and wonders? Is not His grace sufficient, as Paul learned, without signs and wonders?

Timothy suffered *often infirmities*. (1 Timothy 5:23) There was no prayer for healing; he was prescribed wine. Epaphroditus was sick and close to death, yet Paul did not attempt to heal him. He even left Trophimus at Miletum sick. Why did Paul not pray for his healing?

We'll talk more about this when we consider Paul's epistles. For now simply consider ... can we rightly assume that God is operating the same in our present age as He was operating in the days of Acts?

Trail Marker #6
Peter's address (3:13)

The God of our fathers glorifies Jesus, Whom you kill, and Whom God rouses from among the dead ... of which we are witnesses.

<u>Repent</u>, then, and turn about for the erasure of your sins,

So that <u>seasons of refreshing</u> should be coming from the face of the Lord,

And He should <u>dispatch the one</u> fixed upon before for you, Christ Jesus,

Whom heaven must indeed receive <u>until the times of restoration of all.</u>

Remember, Peter is addressing the Israelites. His message; that Jesus was roused from among the dead; was to cause Israel to BELIEVE that Jesus was, in fact, the Son of God and the Christ (Messiah).

And by adding, *What God announces before through the prophets, the suffering of His Christ, He thus fulfills;* Peter is citing the Old Testament Scriptures in support of his argument to Israel.

Notice that following the death and resurrection of Jesus, the message to Israel has not changed. Israel awaits the restoration of the kingdom upon the earth, as in the days of King David.

Jesus proclaimed, *Repent; the kingdom is near.* Peter now proclaims, *Repent; that Christ will return from heaven and seasons of refreshing will be coming.* (In other words, that the kingdom would come upon the earth, as it is in heaven.)

It is important to pause and consider the message being proclaimed at this juncture. If Israel will repent, Christ will return and the kingdom will be restored to Israel.

Milestones as they Awaited the King's Return *(The Waiting)*

++ Some observations along the way ++

Chapter 4. Peter and John are arrested. Many hear the word and believe, and the number of men grows to about 5000.

When questioned about a healing, Peter replies: Let it be known to you and to the entire PEOPLE OF ISRAEL that in the name of Jesus Christ, the Nazarene, Whom you crucify, Whom God rouses from among the dead, in this name the man stands before you sound.

So Peter's remarks are clearly directed to the people of Israel.

They order Peter and John to stop teaching in the name of Jesus. They reply that they must speak of what they had seen and heard.

Chapter 5. Ananias and Sapphira embezzle and lie to God about it. They immediately fall dead. Many signs and miracles occur among the people thru the hands of the apostles.

The apostles are jailed, and then released by a messenger. When challenged as to why they continue teaching in Jesus' name, Peter replies: The God of our fathers rouses Jesus. This *Inaugerator and Saviour* God exalts to His right hand, *to give repentance* TO ISRAEL and the *pardon of sins*.

The Jewish leaders intend to assassinate them, but Gamaliel (a Pharisee in the Sanhedrin and a teacher of the law) advises them to be left alone. *If this work is of men, it will be demolished. But if it is of God, you will not be able to demolish them, lest you may be found fighting against God.*

Chapter 6. Dissension arises in the ecclesia between the Hellenists and the Hebrews. (The Hellenists were Jews that had accepted Greek customs.) The apostles tell the brethren to choose seven proven men to serve. Stephen is one of those chosen.

The word of God grows and the number of disciples in Jerusalem multiplies tremendously.

Stephen is doing great miracles and signs. Jewish leaders claim that he blasphemed Moses and God. Stephen is led before the Sanhedrin and false witnesses take the stand against him.

Chapter 7. After a stirring speech recounting a history of Israel, Stephen is stoned. Saul was one in their midst that endorsed the assassination of Stephen.

Milestones as they Awaited the King's Return *(The Waiting)*

++ Some observations along the way ++

Chapter 8. A great persecution of the ecclesia in Jerusalem arises, and they were dispersed among the districts of Judea and Samaria, except the apostles.

<u>Saul devastated the ecclesia</u>, going into homes to drag out men and women; giving them over to jail. Those who are dispersed evangelize with the word.

Philip evangelizes in Samaria, bringing *the evangel concerning the kingdom of God and the name of Jesus Christ.* (8:12) Many spirits are cast out, and many are cured.

Hearing that Samaria had received the word of God, the apostles in Jerusalem send Peter and John who come and pray so they might obtain the holy spirit. They had been baptized, but the holy spirit had not yet *fallen on any of them.* Peter and John place their hands on them, and they obtain holy spirit.

The villages of the Samaritans are evangelized.

Chapter 9.

> **Trail Marker #7**
>
> # Saul's Conversion (9:1)

On the road to Damascus, Saul is blinded for three days, and does not eat or drink.

A voice from heaven says, *He is a choice instrument of Mine, to bear my name before both the nations and kings, besides the sons of Israel...*

Note the two parts to Paul's commission. He is to bear Christ's name before:

- ✓ Nations and kings (i.e. the nations), and
- ✓ The sons of Israel

Unlike the Twelve who are commissioned to go only to Israel, Paul has a dual commission. He is the ONLY apostle commissioned to go to the nations; but note that he is ALSO commissioned to go to the sons of Israel.

We must keep this in mind as we continue our review of Acts, and when we read Paul's epistles. We must always ask; is this word being spoken to the nations or to Israel?

Paul was commissioned to go to both; and we cannot assume the message he bears will be the same in both cases. In fact we will see huge differences in the message Paul (and the others) proclaims to Israel, and the message Paul proclaim to the nations.

Milestones as they Awaited the King's Return (The Waiting)

Trail Marker #8
Saul's Ministry Begins (9:19)

Saul comes to be with the disciples in Damascus for some days. Immediately in the synagogues he heralds Jesus, that He is the Son of God. The Jews of Damascus are confused as Saul deduces that Jesus is the Christ, and they consult to assassinate him. The disciples lower Saul thru the wall in a hamper. (See 2 Corinthians 11:32)

Coming to Jerusalem Saul spends time with the disciples. (Galatians 1:18-19) He speaks boldly with the Hellenists, and they try to assassinate him. The brethren lead him into Caesarea, and they send him to Tarsus.

From Galatians 1:17 we learn that in these early days Saul went to Arabia and then back to Damascus; before going to Jerusalem. He makes it clear that the evangel he proclaims was not received from men but came thru a revelation of Jesus Christ. (Galatians 1:12)

Had Saul's (Paul's) message been the same as that being declared by the other apostles, he would logically have gone first to spend time with the others ... those that had seen and heard Christ first hand. But he makes it very clear that this was not the case.

Paul's "my evangel" was not just the same message going to a different group of people (the Gentiles). He was entrusted with the evangel *of* the Uncircumcision, while Peter was entrusted with the evangel *of* the Circumcision. (Galatians 2:7)

Milestones as they Awaited the King's Return *(The Waiting)*

++ Some observations along the way ++

The ecclesia throughout Judea, Galilee and Samaria enjoy a time of peace. Their numbers multiply.

Peter heals Eneas, the Paralytic. All those dwelling at Lydda and Saron are aware of him and turn back to the Lord.

Peter then raises Tabitha from the dead. This miracle becomes known in all of Joppa, and many *believe on the Lord*.

Trail Marker #9
Cornelius (10:1)

Chapter 10. Peter is instructed in a vision to go to Cornelius, a centurion who was devout and fearing God, along with his entire house. Peter tells Cornelius, I grasp that God is not partial, but *in every nation he who is fearing Him and acting righteously is acceptable to Him.*

Is Peter now going to the Gentiles?

Observe the shock on the part of the believing Jews (the ecclesia) that a Gentile would receive the holy spirit from God. It was hard for Peter to believe that he should even go to the house of a Gentile and proclaim the evangel to him.

From the time of Abraham it was God's plan to *bless all peoples,* but until now God has worked strictly thru the Jews. Jesus Himself would go only to the sheep of Israel, and "the church" (ecclesia) up to now is also exclusively Jewish.

Everything we have read thus far in Acts has pertained to the JEWISH believers. Has the plan now changed? Will God now go directly to the Gentiles?

Cornelius was no ordinary Gentile. He was devout, feared God, and beseeched God continually. He sought after the God of Abraham, and God now commissions Peter to go to him.

But as we read on, observe that Peter and the other apostles will continue to go exclusively to the Jews. We remember once again Paul's words; that Paul was entrusted with the evangel of the Uncircumcision, while Peter was entrusted with the evangel of the Circumcision. (Galatians 2:7)

Milestones as they Awaited the King's Return *(The Waiting)*

++ Some observations along the way ++

Chapter 11. Peter is criticized for going to the Gentiles. After hearing of Peter's vision, they glorify God, saying, Consequently, to the nations also God gives repentance unto life.

Those who are dispersed evangelize as far as Phoenicia and Cyprus and Antioch, speaking the word to no one except TO THE JEWS ONLY. A vast number who believe turn back to the Lord.

Barnabas and Saul go to Antioch, remaining there with the ecclesia for a year, teaching a considerable throng.

Agabus prophesies a great famine that is about to come upon the whole inhabited earth, which occurred under Claudius.

Chapter 12. A great persecution arises. Herod, the king, assassinates James, the brother of John. Peter is jailed, but then freed by a messenger. Herod dies.

The word of God grows. Barnabas and Saul return from Jerusalem to Antioch, taking along John Mark.

Milestones as they Awaited the King's Return *(The Waiting)*

> ### Trail Marker #10
> # We pause in our journey thru Acts

To this point the believers from among Israel, led by Peter and James, are central to the history recorded in Acts.

Israel once more hears the evangel of the kingdom, but now that message is strengthened by the resurrection of the King who had been crucified. Israel had rejected the kingdom during Jesus' earthly ministry as recorded in the gospel accounts. In Acts the holy spirit descends and the same kingdom message is again proclaimed; but it is rejected once again.

The kingdom had been *locked* during Jesus' earthly ministry, and the keys were given to Peter. In Acts Peter unlocks the kingdom and it is once again proclaimed to Israel. But, sadly, again it is rejected.

Acts is a transition. And from this point forward in Acts we will see a change. Saul (later renamed Paul) will now become primary.

Remember that early in Acts, when Judas was replaced, it was important to keep the number of apostles at twelve. This makes sense since the apostles represented the ecclesia (called-out-ones) from among Israel which was comprised of twelve tribes.

But when Paul assumes the forefront and is named an apostle, this is a new thing. It will be twelve PLUS Paul. This makes sense since Paul is named apostle to the nations. This, too, is a new thing. To this point the nations are only blessed thru Israel. But later, in Paul's writings, we will see that the believers among the nations will be joint heirs, on the same level as Israel.

It is important to *rightly divide* the word of God, not mixing together things that are different. Doing so leads to confusion and a failure to understand that which God is trying to reveal to us.

The Twelve, and the early church (called-out-ones) recorded thus far in Acts are exclusively believers among Israel. We within the Body of Christ today cannot reach back and claim that the events recorded and the words spoken pertain to us today; for this was a time when God was working thru ISRAEL as His channel to bless all people.

With Paul, and especially with his later letters, we will see truths not revealed by the prophets, in the four gospel accounts, or in this first part of Acts.

And so we will pause here with our overview of Acts to look at the letters written by the leaders in Israel; letters written <u>to the believers among Israel</u>. Once we have done this we will return to our study of Acts.

The Circumcision letters are an extension of the kingdom message operative in the first part of Acts, which bears the same message as that proclaimed during Jesus' earthly ministry. *The kingdom is near. Ready yourselves for the kingdom.*

The message is concerned with Israel, upon the earth; whereas the message to the Body of Christ is concerned with all nations, with an expectation in the heavens. Any attempt to mix the messages found within the Circumcision letters with the messages proclaimed to the nations within Paul's writings will only lead to confusion, and a distortion of the message God has for us today.

++ Some observations along the way ++

Hebrews

WARNING! This letter is clearly directed to the Hebrew believers within the early ecclesia, and not to those of the nations or the Body of Christ. All Scripture is for our benefit, but not all Scripture is written directly to us in this present age.

We must take care not to force direct application of this writing into our present context. God clearly deals differently with different people groups (Israel versus non-Israel) and in different eras.

Trail Marker #11
Impossible to renew repentance (6:4)

Once enlightened, if one falls aside it is impossible to renew to repentance.

Remember that this is directed to Hebrew believers, whose expectation was the return of the Messiah to restore the kingdom. In anticipation of this coming kingdom, perseverance was needed to be qualified.

It is interesting that when the called-for repentance does not come, and the coming kingdom is delayed until the complement of the nations enters, (Romans 11:25) God works in a new direction not described in Hebrews. Thru Paul He will announce the Body of Christ, a heavenly expectation not upon this earth, where repentance and perseverance are not requirements. It will be fully the grace and the work of God, lest any man boast.

But in this present context, to the Hebrew believers, perseverance is required, and if one falls back and rejects Christ they will be hardened and it will be impossible to renew to repentance. This one will have forfeited the enjoyment of his allotment in the eon to come.

But he will not and cannot forfeit his ultimate reconciliation with God at the end of the ages.

Milestones as they Awaited the King's Return (The Waiting)

> ### Trail Marker #12
> ## Not forsaking the assembling (10:25)

Not forsaking the assembling of ourselves, according as the custom of some is, but entreating, and so much rather as you are observing the day drawing near.

Again ... this is directed to Israel! They were meeting in synagogues.

Assembling in specific places was always an important thing for Israel, and even commanded by God on the feast days.

Later, in Paul's ministry to the nations, we see no command to assemble at specific places. Often the believers met in homes. There is no record, until later centuries, of believers from among the nations gathering at specific times or in specific places.

There is certainly much to be gained when we meet together. We can encourage one another, and entreat one another toward greater faith and good works. But for us within the Body of Christ in our present day there is no <u>command</u> or <u>instruction</u> to meet together at specific times or places. We can encourage one another within our families, our circle of friends, our work associates, and our neighborhoods.

Worship happens when we revere God, even when we are alone. "Corporate worship" is not commanded for the Body of Christ.

As a matter of fact, those assembling together with other believers within "organized churches" should beware. Much that happens within the life of organized churches is based on the traditions of men and not the word of God. Teachings are often built on the traditions and teachings of men, and not the pure word of God. Much error is taught concerning the will of God.

Traditional churches can provide venues for believers to meet together, but take care not to become contaminated by the traditions of men; just as Jesus once warned those of Israel in the days of His earthly ministry.

James

James was the brother of Jesus. (Matthew 13:55; Mark 6:3) When James is mentioned in Acts 12:17 it is clear he is not the apostle James, for the latter had been killed in Acts 12:2.

James lived in the land of Israel his entire life. In the early part of Acts, Peter is chief among the apostles and was foremost in proclaiming the Circumcision evangel. But as early as Paul's first visit to Jerusalem, James had a prominent place though he was not an apostle. (Galatians 1:19) Fourteen years later he had risen to become one of the *pillars* in Jerusalem and was named before Peter and John. (Galatians 2:9)

Peter became concerned about the teachings of those associated with James. (Galatians 2:12) At the council in Jerusalem to consider the question of requiring those of the nations to be circumcised, James had the decisive word which placed requirements on the nations. (Colossians 2:14) The decree was later nullified as the secret administration was revealed thru Paul. (Ephesians 2:15)

It would seem that as the apostasy increased within the ecclesia and as greater emphasis was placed upon the physical connection to the Lord, James rose in prominence. But Paul repudiates any physical connection to the Lord. (Philippians 3:4-12)

E. W. Bullinger, in *How to Enjoy the Bible,* notes that James' epistle is filled with references to the Sermon on the Mount; also directed specifically to Israel. In fact, Bullinger cites 25 passages in James that relate directly to the Sermon on the Mount.

Milestones as they Awaited the King's Return *(The Waiting)*

> **Trail Marker #13**
>
> ## The address on the envelope (1:1)

James identifies himself as the author and directs the letter *to the* TWELVE TRIBES *in the dispersion.*

If my father were to direct a letter to my brother, I could learn from what is written, but I could not claim any of the specifics as if it were written to me.

When James writes to the twelve tribes who were dispersed because of persecution, we must remember that these are <u>believers from among Israel</u>. Yes, there may be general principles that can be observed, but the specifics were written TO ISRAEL and not to the Body of Christ. We begin with this caution ...

WARNING! This letter is directed to the believing "sheep of Israel" within the early ecclesia, and not to the Body of Christ. All Scripture is for our benefit, but not all Scripture is written directly TO us in this present age.

We must take care not to force direct application of this writing into our present context. God clearly deals differently with different people groups (Israel versus non-Israel) and in different eras.

> ## Trail Marker #14
> ## Justification is NOT by faith alone
> (2:24)

If one proclaims faith but has no works, that faith cannot save him. If a brother or sister needs food or clothing, yet you tell them to go in peace without giving them food or clothing, what is the benefit?

Faith, if it should not have works: it is dead by itself. Show me your faith apart from the works and I shall be showing you my faith by my works. You believe that God is one, but the demons also believe and are shuddering.

You see that by works a man is being justified, and not by faith alone.

<u>This statement directly conflicts with Paul's claim in Romans.</u>

For we are reckoning a man to be justified by faith apart from works of law. (Romans 3:28)

For if Abraham was justified by acts, he has something to boast in ... Abraham believes God, and it is reckoned to him for righteousness. Now to the worker, the wage is not reckoned as a favor, but as a debt. Yet to him who is not working yet is believing on Him ... his faith is reckoned for righteousness. (Romans 4:1-15)

Interestingly, James uses an example from Abraham's life as found in Genesis 22, AFTER he was circumcised and illustrating Abraham's obedience. In Romans 3, Paul uses an example found in Genesis 15 BEFORE Abraham's circumcision that was to do with his spiritual seed, apart from any works.

In Matthew, as Jesus proclaimed the coming kingdom to be restored upon the earth, works is crucial to entrance into the kingdom. In the Circumcision letters (James being one of them) we see the salvation requirement of faith plus works, for the audience (believing Israel) was still being prepared for entry into the kingdom to come upon the earth.

But Paul's evangel was different. He received it directly from the Lord. It was the next step in God's progressive revelation, and works no longer played a part.

Consider the progression. In the Old Testament the requirement was <u>works</u>. For believing Israel the requirement is <u>faith plus works</u>. In both cases the recipients of the word displayed inability in meeting the requirement. Who, then, can be saved? All this to take humanity to the place where it is recognized that only God's grace can save.

Paul proclaimed <u>faith alone</u>, with no works requirement. Yes, ideal acts were called for as a <u>response</u> to God's grace, but not as a <u>requirement</u> for salvation. One without works would be saved, yet as one escaping through fire. (1 Corinthians 3:15)

So we see the importance of recognizing the distinction between the Circumcision evangel, as proclaimed here by James … and the Uncircumcision evangel as proclaimed by Paul. Any who attempt to mix the two messages will be distorting the evangel and preaching A DIFFERENT EVANGEL, as Paul warned of in Galatians 1:6-9.

And the difficulty in reconciling James 2:24 with Romans 3:28 may cause us to discount one or the other, as did Martin Luther who considered James to be an "epistle of straw" and not worthy of being considered Scripture.

Remember that Israel was promised regeneration, but the Body of Christ is a new creation. Paul proclaimed that the Body of Christ believers have died with Christ. No longer in body, they were now reckoned as spirit; a new creation. While the fullness of this fact will not be realized until the resurrection, God *reckons* the Body in this way even at present. Our old creation is gone. We now live in Christ.

So Israel awaits regeneration and will serve the Lord upon the earth, and entrance into the kingdom will require faith plus works. But the Body of Christ is reckoned dead and a new creation, and upon resurrection will serve the Lord in the celestial realm.

And even today, reckoning our old self dead and now living in Christ, the requirement is faith alone.

1 Peter

Peter identifies himself as the writer of this letter. (1:1) Peter was chief among the twelve apostles throughout Jesus' earthly ministry, and we recall that the ministry of the apostles was directed *exclusively to the sheep of Israel*. (Matthew 10:6;15:24)

Even after Christ's resurrection Peter addressed only *the house of Israel*. (Acts 2:14-36) In Acts we see Peter as the foundation on which the Circumcision ecclesia (believers from among Israel) was built. He remained chief of the twelve until superseded by the Lord's brother James in the Pentecostal era.

Peter was given the keys to the kingdom, (Matthew 16:19) and it was the kingdom to be restored unto Israel upon the earth that he proclaimed. Baptism and repentance continually accompanied the proclamation of the kingdom, or the Circumcision evangel.

Paul tells us that he had been entrusted with the *evangel of the Uncircumcision,* and Peter had been entrusted with the *evangel of the Circumcision*. (Galatians 2:7) He did not say that his was the evangel TO the Uncircumcision; but OF the Uncircumcision. It was A DIFFERENT MESSAGE, and this can be clearly seen if we examine the details.

Whereas Paul addressed the ecclesia (church) which is Christ's Body, Peter writes to *a chosen race, a royal priesthood, a holy nation*.

WARNING! Peter's letter is directed to the believing "sheep of Israel" within the early ecclesia, and not to the Body of Christ.

We must *correctly cut,* or *rightly divide,* the word of truth. (2 Timothy 2:15)

In contrast to Paul who was a persecutor of Christ and of believers, Peter was a devout and obedient Israelite. He wrote *to the chosen expatriates of the dispersion of Pontus, Galatia, Cappadocia, the province of Asia, and Bithynia* (1 Peter 1:1) This clearly ties Peter's writings to the Circumcision (Israel), as the Gentiles were never dispersed to Asia Minor from their own land. It was the Jewish Christians that were forced to flee at the time of Stephen's stoning.

Believing Israel finds itself in the midst of persecution and suffering, probably during the reign of Nero when Christians were tortured and killed routinely. Peter's writings have no direct application for us in this era, as

Milestones as they Awaited the King's Return *(The Waiting)*

Paul's evangel of the Uncircumcision and his revelations of the mysteries previously hidden now pertain. But Peter's epistles will be a great comfort to those among Israel facing terrible persecutions in the days preceding the Lord's return to restore the kingdom; which we read of in Revelation.

Believing the Lord's return was near, Peter wrote to encourage them as they endured suffering, pointing to the expectation that lay before them. And he encouraged them to persevere and remain obedient, living holy (set apart) lives, exhibiting behavior in contrast to that of the nations.

Milestones as they Awaited the King's Return (The Waiting)

> Trail Marker #15
> ## A holy priesthood (2:4)

As the Lord was rejected by men yet chosen by God and held in honor, you also as living stones are being built up a spiritual house, into a holy priesthood, to offer up spiritual sacrifices, most acceptable to God through Jesus Christ.

Priesthood = Israel.

Consider Paul's word to the Body of Christ. There is one mediator – Christ. (1 Timothy 2:5) There is no room for a priesthood in Paul's words. All are parts of the Body. All are Christ's ambassadors, not priests. (2 Corinthians 5:18-21)

Clearly Peter speaks to a different audience, with words that resonate with believing Israel. They are priests, and they will serve as God's mediators to humanity in the final eons upon the earth after Christ's return.

It is *believing* Israel that has the honor, for the unbelieving are as a stone rejected by the builder; stumbling and stubborn. (2:7) *Yet you are a chosen race, a "royal priesthood," a "holy nation."* (2:9) This clearly fits Israel, for what other nation could be referred to as a *holy* nation?

And what is the purpose of the holy priesthood?

... so that you should be recounting the virtues of Him Who calls you out of darkness into His marvelous light, who once were "not a people" yet now are the people of God, who "have not enjoyed mercy," yet now are "being showed mercy." (2:9)

This is a direct reference to Hosea 1:9-11 which clearly speaks of Israel, and not of the nations.

The purpose of the priesthood is to display to humanity God's virtues, and this will surely take place in the final eons upon the earth when believing Israel will serve as God's priesthood. Once exiled and scattered and not a nation nor a people, once again upon being restored will Israel be a nation and a people for the purpose of recounting God's virtues to humanity.

2 Peter

Trail Marker #16
As Paul writes to you (3:15)

... in which some things are hard to apprehend. The unlearned and unstable are twisting.

We remember that Paul was commissioned to go to those of Israel and *also* those of the nations. (Acts 9:15) In Acts we see him beginning in the synagogues, and when he is expelled he then goes to those of the nations.

Paul's later epistles are addressed primarily to those within the Body of Christ, or the ecclesia comprised of Jews and Gentiles with no distinction or preference. But somewhere along the way Paul directed a letter to those of Israel, as Peter mentions here.

Some speculate that Hebrews was written by Paul, although its author is not revealed in the letter. Whether Paul wrote Hebrews or not, it is clear from Peter's comments here that Paul did address the believers among Israel at some point.

Also note the words, *as the rest of the scriptures also.* (v. 16) Paul's writings are here spoken of by Peter as *scriptures*.

John 1,2,3

There is no address on John's first letter. The second is addressed, *From the Elder; to the chosen lady and her children whom I am loving in truth.* This is a bit cryptic. Was John using a code, due to the persecution the believers faced? Was he simply being poetic?

We can only speculate as to his reasons. But from the context and the many similarities in word and phrase structure with John's gospel, clearly the writer is the apostle John.

The third letter is addressed, *From the Elder; to Gaius, the beloved.* But again we see many similarities to John's gospel ... light vs. darkness, the Word, the Light. And reference is made to the transfiguration of Christ, to which only the apostles Peter, James and John were witnesses.

In every recorded instance, John's ministry is limited to the Circumcision (Israel). He views the nations as being outside of his scope. (3 John 5-8) He makes a distinction between *ours* (Israel) and the whole world. (1 John 2:2) He places great emphasis on his personal connection with Jesus during His earthly ministry. (1 John 1:1-4)

At the Jerusalem conference, James, Cephas (Peter) and John represent the Circumcision, and Paul the Uncircumcision. (Galatians 2:6-9) In that instance John, along with James and Peter, are referred to as *pillars* within the ecclesia of Jewish believers.

We remember that during Christ's kingdom ministry the nations are blessed only thru Israel. We see this expressed in John's gospel and letters; in God's love for the world. (John 3:16)

WARNING! *We must correctly cut, or rightly divide, the word of truth.* (2 Timothy 2:15)

John's letters are directed to the believing "sheep of Israel" within the early ecclesia, and not to the Body of Christ.

All Scripture is for our benefit, but not all Scripture is written directly TO us in this present age. We must take care not to force direct application of this writing into our present context. God clearly deals differently with different people groups (Israel versus the nations) and in different eras.

Milestones as they Awaited the King's Return (The Waiting)

> Trail Marker #17
> ## A growing apostasy (2:27)

The anointing you received from Him remains in you, and you have no need that anyone may be teaching you. His anointing is teaching you concerning all.

As apostasy grew within the ecclesia some teachers were apparently responsible for the turning away. John's audience is encouraged not to trust teachers (for they might be misled), but to be led by the holy spirit.

The ecclesia was not growing stronger, but was weakening with this apostasy; to the point where the flock could no longer trust teachers and needed to rely directly on the holy spirit for truth.

Diotrephes, fond of being foremost among the ecclesia, is not receiving us. If I come I will remind him of his acts; gossiping about us with wicked words and casting the brethren out of the ecclesia. (3 John 9)

This is perhaps the reason John wrote this letter. Diotrephes has allowed pride to take hold as he leads the ecclesia. He is fond of being foremost. He gossips about the apostle. He is casting brethren out of the ecclesia, clearly without good reason (else John would not find fault with him doing so).

Clearly the apostasy ... the "falling away" ... was growing!

Jude

Jude (Judas) tells us he is a brother of James, and therefore the brother of Jesus. Remember that James was prominent among the Circumcision believers (Israel).

This letter is directed to the believing "sheep of Israel" within the early ecclesia, and not to the Body of Christ.

Jude is a prelude to Revelation. The central theme is the coming of the Lord in judgment on the irreverent. (v. 14-15)

Milestones as they Awaited the King's Return *(The Waiting)*

Summary of "The Waiting"

Throughout the four gospel accounts we see a distinctive Jewish focus. We find many Old Testament references. Jesus announces the restoration of the kingdom.

But the king and the kingdom are rejected by the Jews who so anxiously awaited their coming, and the king is crucified.

Still, the evangel remains the same in the book of Acts when Peter (who was given the keys to the kingdom) proclaims the same message. Christ has been crucified and resurrected, but in the book of Acts it is still the kingdom to come upon the earth that is being proclaimed, and it is proclaimed exclusively to the Jews as was the case throughout Matthew. Salvation, or life in the eon to come, is life in the kingdom of the heavens when it comes upon the earth with Christ upon the throne.

The believers among Israel were awaiting the return of Christ. And as they awaited this event, the circumcision epistles addressed them; encouraging them to endure, even thru times of persecution. Remain true to the faith; and beware of false teachers that would mislead!

Throughout Acts we see the evangel of the kingdom continually rejected. When the kingdom is *finally* rejected at the end of Acts, the Jews (and the kingdom evangel) are set aside for a season and the uncircumcision evangel is declared by Paul to Jew and Gentile alike without distinction or preference.

But have the Jews lost their chance? Has "The Church" taken their place?

Paul tells us that Israel has been calloused UNTIL *the complement of the nations may be entering,* after which time *all Israel shall be saved.* (Romans 11:25)

When this present age has ended the kingdom evangel will once again be proclaimed upon the earth, and we see this happen in Revelation.

Milestones in Paul's Ministry
"The Pause"

An Overview of the Scriptures, by
BOB EVELY © 2018.
An Independent Minister of Christ Jesus,
Of the church at Wilmore, Kentucky

Now that we have considered the first part of Acts and the Circumcision letters, all of which were focused on believers from among Israel, we come to a turning point.

Israel has rejected her king and crucified Him. Peter continues with the same message to Israel; repent and ready yourselves for the coming kingdom. But once again resistance appears and this kingdom message is rejected.

God now does something not foretold by the prophets, who had foreseen the re-gathering of Israel and the restoration of the kingdom. With the rejection of the kingdom message there is now a *pause* in that agenda.

The kingdom will still be restored, and the apostles and the writers of the Circumcision letters instruct the Jewish believers to persevere and wait for that restoration. But in the meantime God will begin a new thing. Saul, who had persecuted and terrorized the believers, and who should rightfully have been struck down, will find grace and a special calling from God.

Let us resume our walk thru Acts.

Acts (Part 2)

We will not detail Saul's conversion and the beginning of his ministry, as we touched on that when thinking about Acts part 1.

But we will observe once again that his early ministry did not begin with Paul studying under the Twelve. His calling is different (grace), his message is different (the evangel of the Uncircumcision), and the audience he is sent to is different (the Jew first; but then the Gentile). God revealed things to Paul that had not been previously revealed (secrets) as Israel is temporarily set aside and as God, thru Paul, go directly to those of the nations.

Milestones in Paul's Ministry *(The Pause)*

++ Some observations along the way ++

Chapter 13. Saul and Barnabas are SEVERED *for the work to which I have called them.*

To SEVER would be to *cut* Saul and Barnabas apart from others in the ecclesia. Had they been taking the same message to the same people (Israel) there would be no need to *sever* them.

We come to our first stopping point ...

> ## Trail Marker #1
> ## In the synagogues (13:5)

Saul and Barnabas begin their first journey (13:4-14:28). At Salamis they announce the word of God *in the synagogues*.

Remember Paul's dual commission from Acts 9; the nations AND Israel. In the first part of Acts, and consistent with Jesus' earthly ministry as described in the gospel accounts, God's word went exclusively to Israel. Now Paul has been commissioned to go to Israel and ALSO to the nations.

But observe that he will go FIRST to Israel (e.g. announcing the word of God in the synagogues where Israel is assembled) and only then, when he is rejected he will go to the nations.

Trail Marker #2
Sergius Paul and Elymas (13:6)

Elymas the Magician (Bar-Jesus) is a false prophet, a Jew. He is with the proconsul Sergius Paul, an intelligent man. Sergius Paul calls for Barnabas and Saul, seeking to hear the word of God. Elymas withstands them, *seeking to pervert the proconsul from the faith.*

Saul, *who is also Paul,* challenges Elymas. Will you not cease perverting the straight ways of the Lord? *You shall be blind, not observing the sun* UNTIL THE APPOINTED TIME. The procounsul believes, astonished at the teaching of the Lord.

This is a picture of the stubbornness of Israel, with the Word subsequently going to the nations.

Elymas, a Jew, seeks to stop the word of God from going to Sergius Paul, a Gentile. It seems that this single case is representative of the Jews and Gentiles as a whole.

Paul will later say, *Callousness, in part, on Israel has come, until the complement of the nations may be entering* (Romans 11:25).

Blindness came upon Elymas so that Sergius Paul of the nations might enter. But observe that this blindness is not permanent, but until the appointed time (in the case of Elymas) and until the complement of the nations may be entering (in the case of Israel as a whole).

Observe also ... when blindness comes to a Jew that salvation might come to a Gentile, we are told that Saul *is also Paul.* Saul is his Hebrew name. Paul is the Gentile name given to him by God. From this point on Saul will be referred to as Paul.

Milestones in Paul's Ministry *(The Pause)*

++ Some observations along the way ++

In Perga, John Mark departs from them and returns to Jerusalem.

Could Mark's departure have been linked to Paul taking the word directly to a Gentile? When Paul prepares to leave on his second journey he will refuse to take John Mark along (Acts 15:37).

On to Antioch, Pisidia ... and Paul is given opportunity to speak in the synagogue. He addresses the *Israelites and those who are fearing God.*

Paul is invited back on the next sabbath, and almost the entire city gathered to hear him. But the Jews contradict him. Paul replies:

To you first was it necessary that the word of God be spoken. Yet, since, in fact, you are thrusting it away, and are judging yourselves not worthy of eonian life, we are turning to the nations.

For thus the Lord has directed us: I have appointed thee for a light of the nations; for thee to be for salvation as far as the limits of the earth.

The nations rejoice and glorify the word of the Lord, and believe, *whoever were set for life eonian.*

Observe the pattern Paul follows. He goes first to the Jews: *To you first was it necessary that the word of God be spoken.* And when he is rejected he turns to the nations.

Milestones in Paul's Ministry *(The Pause)*

++ More observations along the way ++

Paul goes thru the whole country, but the Jews rouse up persecution for Paul and Barnabas. They eject them from their boundaries, and they move on to Iconium.

Chapter 14. In Iconium a vast multitude of Jews and Greeks believe. Stubborn Jews oppose them, but they remain a considerable time. Signs and miracles testify to the word of His grace, but ultimately they are pelted with stones and forced to flee.

Paul heals a lame man, and they think Paul and Barnabas are gods (Hermes and Zeus).

The Jews follow Paul and stone him, dragging him outside the city thinking he is dead. Surrounded by disciples Paul rises.

On to Derbe where the evangelize and make a considerable number of disciples. They then backtrack and return into Lystra, Iconium and Antioch; entreating them to remain in the faith.

They proceed to Pisidia, Pamphylia, Perga, Attalia; and they then return to Antioch. There they gather the ecclesia and inform them of what God does with them, and that He opens to the nations a door of faith.

Chapter 15. Judaizers follow after Paul, teaching the brethren they must be circumcised to be saved. They prescribe that Paul, Barnabas and some others are to go up to the apostles and elders in Jerusalem concerning this question.

Milestones in Paul's Ministry *(The Pause)*

> ### Trail Marker #3
> # Jerusalem Council (15:4)

They are received by the ecclesia, apostles and elders, and inform them of what God does with them.

Some from the sect of the Pharisees who believe rise up, insisting they must be circumcised and must keep the law of Moses. Peter objects:

Why are you trying to place on them a yoke which neither our fathers nor we are strong enough to bear? Thru the grace of the Lord Jesus we are believing, to be saved in a manner even as they.

So Peter observes that salvation is not found by observing the law, as the Jews had found it impossible to do since the time the law was given. Salvation, for Jew and Gentile alike, comes thru believing. Belief comes thru the grace of the Lord Jesus, and salvation follows belief.

Barnabas and Paul tell of the signs and miracles God does among the nations thru them.

James then addresses the group. *Wherefore I decide not to harass those from the nations, but write a letter to them; to be abstaining from ceremonial pollution with idols, and prostitution, and what is strangled, and blood. For Moses has those heralding him, being read on every sabbath in the synagogues.*

Consider James' decision! While Peter addressed the council, it appears that James had authority to make the final decision on behalf of the Jewish ecclesia (15:19).

While Peter advised that no yoke be placed upon the Gentile believers, it seems that James' decision was a bit of a compromise. While he basically agreed with Peter, still he took a few things from the law and insisted upon them as *essentials*. His reasoning is given in 15:21, so as not to create a stumbling block for those that were hearing the law of Moses proclaimed on every sabbath. Still, James declared certain "essential" portions from the law to be added to the grace of the Lord.

Milestones in Paul's Ministry *(The Pause)*

While we understand James' reasoning, was he correct in imposing these *essentials* upon the Gentile believers?

Another consideration ... Did Paul "submit" to Jerusalem? It would seem at first that Paul was *required* to appear before the apostles and elders in Jerusalem to defend his position. But when we read Paul's account in Galatians 2:2 we see that he went voluntarily, *in accord with a revelation,* and there he *submitted to them the evangel which I am heralding among the nations, yet privately to those of repute, lest somehow I should be racing or ran for naught.*

Paul was not subservient to the leaders in Jerusalem. He was an apostle in his own right, chosen by God as His instrument to be a light to the nations.

As they pass thru the cities they relay the Jerusalem decree. But did Paul agree with the decree?

The decision by James at the Jerusalem council and the resulting epistle being circulated among the ecclesias was, at least to James, a "decree" which delineated certain "essentials" for the brethren. Paul seems to go along with the decree, but it is clear from his writings that he did not consider these things to be "essentials" as it pertains to salvation.

Paul does say that to the Jews he became as a Jew (1 Corinthians 9:20) to be gaining Jews. But while the Jerusalem decree required abstaining from idol sacrifices, Paul points out in 1 Corinthians 8 that there is really nothing wrong with eating meat that was tied to idol sacrifices.

But he does go on to say, *Beware lest somehow this right of yours may become a stumbling block to the weak.* (1 Corinthians 8:9) If one exercises his freedom, and this results in injury to others, he is *sinning against brethren* and *sinning against Christ.* (1 Corinthians 8:12)

It seems from Paul's writings that he would not agree that the items in the Jerusalem Decree were "essentials," except in cases where exercising freedoms would cause a stumbling block to others.

Milestones in Paul's Ministry *(The Pause)*

++ Some observations along the way ++

The apostles, elders and the whole ecclesia choose men to send along with Paul and Barnabas. They send Judas (called Bar-Sabbas) and Silas.

A letter is sent with these representatives; not to be placing one more burden on believers except these essentials; to be abstaining from idol sacrifices, and blood, and what is strangled, and prostitution.

They return to Antioch.

They depart for the second journey (15:36-18:23) to visit the brethren at every city where the word of the Lord was announced, to see how they are faring.

But Paul refuses to take John Mark along, creating a disturbance with Barnabas. Barnabas takes John Mark and heads for Cyprus, while Paul chooses Silas to accompany him.

Does this display a transition in Paul's ministry?

Paul had been travelling with Barnabas (a fellow Jew), but because of the disagreement over John Mark, Barnabas departs from Paul. Paul's new companion, Silas, is a Gentile. Could this be symbolic, following the Jerusalem council, of Paul's gradual movement from his ministry to the Jews toward his ministry to the Gentiles? Paul is the apostle to the Gentiles, but remember his commission was to both Jew and Gentile (Acts 9:15) and he has typically gone first into the synagogues.

++

On they travel to Syria, Cilicia, Derbe and Lystra.

Chapter 16. Paul is joined by Timothy, the son of a believing Jewish woman and a Greek father.

Paul circumcises Timothy *because of the Jews who are in those places, for they all were aware that his father belonged to the Greeks.*

Paul continues to maintain that circumcision is not necessary, but knowing that he is still going into the synagogues he wishes to remove any possible stumbling block. (See Paul's message concerning the use of freedoms that could be stumbling blocks to others in 1 Corinthians 8:9ff.)

Milestones in Paul's Ministry *(The Pause)*

++ More observations along the way ++

Paul encounters Lydia. The Lord opens up her heart to heed what is spoken by Paul. She and her household are baptized.

Observe that it is not Lydia's free will that enables her to believe the message spoken by Paul. The Lord opened her heart to heed the message.

Paul casts a spirit from a diviner. The spirit had brought a vast income to the woman's master, so they take Paul and Silas to the magistrates and they are cast into jail. A great quake opens the prison doors and they are freed.

Chapter 17. In Thessalonica Paul enters the synagogues and on three sabbaths he argues from the scriptures that Jesus is the Christ.

In Berea Paul goes into the synagogue of the Jews. The Bereans are more noble than those in Thessalonica; they search the Scriptures. Many believe, including not a few of the respectable Greeks.

Jews from Thessalonica come and agitate the throngs. Paul is sent away by the brethren, while Silas and Timothy remain behind.

Milestones in Paul's Ministry *(The Pause)*

> ### Trail Marker #4
> ### Before the Areopagus (17:19)

In Athens, philosophers lead Paul to the Areopagus asking, Can we know what this new teaching is? Paul addresses the Areopagus.

<u>*I behold how religious you are*</u>, *noting the inscription: "To an Unknowable God." This One am I announcing to you; the God Who makes the world and all that is in it. He is not dwelling in temples made by hands. He is not attended by human hands and is not requiring anything. He gives to all life and breath and all. He makes out of one every nation of mankind. He specifies the setting of the seasons and the bounds of their dwelling, for them to be seeking God. Not far from each of us is He inherent. In Him we are living and moving.* <u>*As your poets declare:*</u> *For of that race also are we. We ought not to be inferring that the Divine is like gold, silver, stone, a sculpture of art and human sentiment.*

Paul's approach before the Areopagus is an excellent model for us! When Paul went into the synagogues, he argued with the Jews from the Scriptures. Why? Because the Jews respected the Scriptures and accepted that they were a revelation from God.

But the Gentiles did not have the same view of Scripture. And here, before the Areopagus, Paul does not argue from the Scriptures. As a matter of fact when Paul does use a direct quote in support of his argument, the quote comes from Gentile poetry and not from Scripture.

Furthermore, Paul does not condemn his audience as pagans, even though his spirit was *incited* when he first arrived in Athens when he saw the many idols. Instead, Paul builds bridges to his audience. He even compliments them, beholding how "religious" they are.

Paul was Christ's Ambassador, and he tailored his approach depending on his audience. *To all have I become all, that I should undoubtedly be saving some.* (1 Corinthians 9:22)

Milestones in Paul's Ministry *(The Pause)*

++ Some observations along the way ++

Chapter 18. In Corinth, the Jews resist and blaspheme, and Paul tells them: *From now on I shall go to the nations.*

Paul enters the house of Titus Justus who is revering God, and whose house is adjacent to the synagogue. Crispis, chief of the synagogue, believes, with his household. Many Corinthians believe and are baptized.

They travel on to Syria, Ephesus (where Paul *argues with the Jews* in the synagogue), Caesarea and Antioch.

They depart on the third journey (18:23-21:16). They travel to the Galatian province and to Phrygia; *establishing all the disciples.*

Trail Marker #5
Apollos corrected by Priscilla & Aquila (18:24)

Apollos is a scholarly man, able in the scriptures. He is instructed in the way of the Lord, fervent in spirit, and he speaks and teaches accurately what concerns Jesus. But he is versed only in the baptism of John.

Priscilla and Aquila expound the way of God to him more accurately. He strenuously and thoroughly confutes the Jews in public, exhibiting thru the scriptures that Jesus is the Christ.

Apollos was teaching *accurately* concerning Jesus. He did have the facts right, but he was only versed in John's baptism and not in truths revealed thereafter.

Here we see a great illustration of the need to "rightly divide" the Scriptures.

Many today are preaching the message of John the Baptist; Repent, for the kingdom is near. That is certainly an accurate message, as these words were declared by Jesus Himself and by His apostles.

But they were declared TO ISRAEL (not the nations) and they pertained to the specific day in which the words were uttered. Let us not, within the Body of Christ today, be versed only in the baptism of John! God has moved on from those truths.

No longer water baptism; but baptism of the spirit. No longer things of the flesh; but spiritual things. No longer GOING to the synagogues on the sabbaths but BEING the Body of Christ in all places and circumstances.

Let us be sure to distinguish between Biblical truths spoken to Israel in a previous era and Biblical truths intended for us today.

Milestones in Paul's Ministry *(The Pause)*

++ Some observations along the way ++

They proceed to Ephesus.

Chapter 19. In the synagogue Paul speaks boldly for three months, arguing and persuading that which concerns the kingdom of God. Some are hardened and stubborn, saying evil things concerning *the way*.

Paul withdraws and *severs the disciples,* arguing day by day in the school of Tyrannus for two years so all in the province of Asia hear the word of the Lord. God does powerful deeds thru Paul.

So Paul continues his custom, going first to the synagogue. When he is rejected he goes to the Gentiles. But he has not yet ceased going first to the Jews.

Milestones in Paul's Ministry *(The Pause)*

> **Trail Marker #6**
> ## Demetrius the Silversmith (19:23)

Demetrius stirs up a group against Paul, pointing out that he is hurting their business in all of Asia, associated with the temples of Artemis. They point out that the sanctuary of the great goddess Artemis is being reckoned nothing.

The mob becomes full of fury; "Great is Artemis of the Ephesians." They apprehend Paul's associates, Gaius and Aristarchus.

The ECCLESIA is in confusion. The majority is not aware why they had come together. They unite on Alexander, one of the throng, and he speaks to the mob.

You must possess composure and not commit anything rash. These men are not despoilers of the sanctuary, nor blasphemers of our goddess. If any has a charge against them, court sessions are to be held, and there are proconsuls.

In the legal ECCLESIA will it be explained. And Alexander dismisses THE ECCLESIA.

Ecclesia is translated "church" in most every case in our modern translations. Here we see *ecclesia* used three times where it certainly cannot mean "church." (Acts 19:32,40,41) Even the modern translators use another word here. *Ecclesia* simply means a group of people "called-out" from a larger group (ek = out; klesia = called).

Ecclesia does not always mean the same thing, as is clearly displayed in the current example. We cannot, therefore, assume the *ecclesia* (church) Jesus spoke of in the Gospels, or the *ecclesia* (church) referred to early in Acts (which was exclusively Jewish), is the same as the *ecclesia* (church) Paul later speaks of.

When we read of the *ecclesia* in God's Word, we should always ask <u>which</u> *ecclesia* (which group of people) is being referred to. We cannot simply take all cases where *ecclesia* is used and use this as the model for our present-day "church."

Milestones in Paul's Ministry *(The Pause)*

++ Some observations along the way ++

Chapter 20. They travel to Macedonia and then Greece, where they spend three months. The Jews plot against Paul and he plans to return thru Macedonia.

On to Philippi. After the days of Unleavened Bread they journey to Troas where they stay for seven days.

Eutychus falls from a third story window. Paul tells them not to worry, for his soul is in him.

From Miletus, Paul calls for *the elders of the ecclesia* in Ephesus.

I am not making my soul precious to myself, till I should be perfecting my career and the dispensation which I got from the Lord Jesus, to certify the evangel of the grace of God.

You shall be seeing my face no longer. Under no circumstances do I shrink from informing you of the entire counsel of God. The holy spirit appointed you supervisors to be shepherding the ecclesia of God.

I am committing you to God and to the word of His grace which is able to edify and give the enjoyment of an allotment among all who have been hallowed.

Chapter 21. They travel to Jerusalem.

Milestones in Paul's Ministry *(The Pause)*

> Trail Marker #7
> ## In Jerusalem (21:20)

They say to Paul, Tens of thousands there are among the <u>Jews who have believed</u>, and all are inherently <u>zealous for the law</u>. They hear that you teach the Jews apostasy from Moses. A multitude must come together, for they will hear you have come.

Go with these four men having a vow on them; be purified with them; all will know what they have heard of you is nothing; that you are observing the elements and you yourself are maintaining the law. Paul does as they instruct him.

Consider Paul's enemies as he enters Jerusalem! We can understand that the non-believing Jews would be his enemies. They objected to Paul's preaching in the name of Jesus. But Paul has other enemies in Jerusalem as well. Here we see that the *Jews who have believed* and who are *zealous for the law* are in an outrage over his teachings. As Paul enters Jerusalem, then, it appears that nearly ALL are against him.

This should lead us to ask; at this point is there a single *ecclesia* of God or are there two? We read in 21:20 that there are the Jewish believers that expect Paul to observe "the elements" and maintain "the law." But they did not expect this of the Gentile believers. Of the Gentiles they expected only that they guard themselves from idol sacrifice, blood, what is strangled, and prostitution. (21:25)

In modern translations the word *ecclesia* is simply translated "church" as if there is only one homogenized group. But here we see that there were actually two distinct groups; the Jewish *ecclesia* and the Gentile *ecclesia;* and there were different expectations for each. Remember Paul's comment in Galatians 2:7; that he had been entrusted with the *evangel of the Uncircumcision* while Peter was entrusted with the *evangel of the Circumcision.*

There were two evangels, for two different groups; and this accounts for the friction between Paul and the Jewish believers.

Milestones in Paul's Ministry *(The Pause)*

We must be very careful to observe, when reading the epistles in the Word of God, WHO they are written to. Peter and the others of the Twelve were writing to the Jewish believers. Paul was writing to the Jewish believers, but also the Gentiles that came into the *ecclesia* by faith (Body of Christ). We have no right to mix the two, or as Gentiles to claim things directed to the Jewish believers!

Milestones in Paul's Ministry *(The Pause)*

++ Some observations along the way ++

Paul is apprehended. He is given permission to speak to the people.

Chapter 22. Paul addresses the crowd. After telling of his Damascus experience he concludes by telling them the instruction he received from Christ Jesus. *You shall be His witness to all men of what you see and hear. I shall be delegating you afar to the nations.* At this word they raise their voice against him, saying it is not befitting for him to live.

It is interesting that they did not object when he proclaims to them that concerning Jesus. Instead they object when Paul says, *"I am going to the nations."* The Jews who had gathered could very well have included those of the Jewish ecclesia that believed in Jesus, but their objection is that Paul is going to the Gentiles.

Milestones in Paul's Ministry *(The Pause)*

++ More observations along the way ++

Chapter 23. Paul addresses the Sanhedrin. A commotion arises between the Pharisees and Sadducees. Fearing for Paul's life the captain orders the troops to snatch him out of their midst, to lead him into the citadel.

They plot to kill Paul, asking the chief priests and elders to have Paul led into an ambush. When the captain learns of the plot he arranges to escort Paul in the night with heavy guard to Caesarea; to the governor Felix.

Chapter 24. Felix gives Paul a hearing, and he postpones to become more acquainted with that which concerns "the way." Felix hears him concerning the faith in Christ Jesus. They argue concerning righteousness, self-control, and the impending judgment.

Festus succeeds Felix. The chief priests and foremost of the Jews inform Festus against Paul. Asking Paul to be brought to Jerusalem, they plan an ambush along the way to kill him. Festus invites Paul's accusers to come to Caesarea.

Chapter 25. Festus hears Paul. Paul insists on being heard at the dais of Caesar.

Chapter 26. King Agrippa hears Paul. They agree that Paul has done nothing deserving of death or bonds, and that he could have been released if he had not appealed to Caesar.

Chapter 27. They travel toward Rome. The ship is caught in a hurricane. Paul tells them not one soul will be cast away, as reported to him by a messenger. There were 276 in the ship.

Chapter 28. Shipwrecked at Melita, a viper bites Paul, but he does not die. They say he is a god. The father of Publius is healed, and others on the island having infirmities come and are cured.

Milestones in Paul's Ministry *(The Pause)*

> Trail Marker #8
> ## Paul addresses the Jews (28:17)

In Rome, Paul calls together those who are foremost of the Jews. Because of the expectation of Israel this chain is about me.

They ask to hear what Paul has to say. On a set day, more come to him in the lodging and Paul expounds from morning till dusk concerning Jesus, both from the law of Moses and the prophets.

Some are persuaded, yet others disbelieve. There being disagreements, they are dismissed. Paul tells them: The holy spirit speaks thru Isaiah to your fathers. You will be hearing but not understanding. You will be observing but not perceiving. For stoutened is the heart of this people.

Let it be known to you, then, that TO THE NATIONS *was dispatched this salvation of God, and they will hear.* (28:28)

This is the same passage from Isaiah that Jesus quoted in Matthew 13:14 as the kingdom evangel was being rejected and He began to speak to the masses only using parables. After the King Himself was rejected (crucified) we read throughout Acts that the kingdom evangel is again proclaimed, and again rejected. Several times Paul has said he would go to the Gentiles, and he then did so. Paul never stopped, however, going to the Jews as well.

Now, however, the Acts of the Apostles has come to a close. We read once again that because of the "stoutened heart" of the Jewish people, salvation is going to the Gentiles. Paul continues to herald the kingdom of God to the end (28:31), but we read his assessment of Israel in Romans 11:25; *Callousness, in part, on Israel has come, until the complement of the nations may be entering. And thus all Israel shall be saved.*

In other words; the coming of the Kingdom upon the earth, to Israel, is postponed, while God's salvation now goes to the nations.

This is a turning point!

Consider; Peter had pleaded in Acts 3 with the *men of Israel* to *turn again* in order that Christ might be sent (3:12-21). Now Paul declares, using the words of Isaiah, that stubborn Israel's eyes would be closed lest they should turn again (28:25-27).

In Acts 13 we read that it was to Israel that the Word of salvation was sent (13:26,40). But now we read that the salvation of God is sent unto the Gentiles (28:28).

And lastly, Paul tells us here that it is for the hope of Israel he had been imprisoned (28:20). But in a later revelation we are told he was the prisoner of Jesus Christ for the Gentiles (Ephesians 3:1-3).

All of this points to the fact that here, at the end of Acts, is a turning point. Always the word had gone to Israel; but now it will go to the Gentiles.

Milestones in Paul's Ministry *(The Pause)*

++ Some observations along the way ++

Paul remains in Rome for two years. He welcomes all those coming to him; heralding the kingdom of God and teaching that which concerns the Lord Jesus Christ with all boldness, unforbidden.

Whereas in 28:23 Paul proclaimed *the law and the prophets*, after this final rejection by the Jews there is no similar mention; but only the kingdom of God. Paul would always go first to Israel, and only to the nations as he was rejected. Now, with this final rejection, the stage is set for Paul's proclamations concerning the Body of Christ, with no preference to Israel. We see the higher truths revealed to Paul in his prison epistles which were written later in his ministry.

Milestones in Paul's Ministry *(The Pause)*

++ More observations along the way ++

Summary of Acts

As we have seen, Acts has two distinct parts. In part one, Peter is primary and his ministry (and that of the other apostles and leaders) is exclusively to Israel. Near the end of part one we see Peter's influence beginning to fade and James appears to take the primary role in leading the Jewish ecclesia. But everything relates exclusively to Israel.

Then comes part two, beginning with the conversion of Saul on the road to Damascus. Saul (Paul) is commissioned to proclaim the evangel to believers of Israel; but he is ALSO commissioned to proclaim to kings and nations aside from Israel.

Throughout Acts, though, he goes first to the synagogues to proclaim to those of Israel, and when he is rejected he goes to those of the nations. Clearly his message is different, which leads to his coming to Jerusalem to explain what he is doing.

We clearly see Peter and the others from the Jerusalem ecclesia proclaiming to the believers among Israel the *Circumcision evangel* that was entrusted to Peter. And Paul, entrusted with the *Uncircumcision evangel,* goes to the nations. And it is not until Acts ends, and when Paul writes his later letters, that we see some of the amazing new truths God has in store for the Body of Christ.

So, as we turn to Paul's letters let us keep in mind his dual commission; to Israel; and to the nations. We must therefore seek to understand from the context of his letters to which group he is speaking.

Romans

Milestones in Paul's Ministry (The Pause)

> Trail Marker #9
> ## The evangel (1:15)

I am eager to bring *the evangel* to you. I am *not ashamed* of the evangel. *It is God's power for salvation to everyone who is believing; to the Jew first, and to the Greek as well. For a righteousness which is of God is being revealed in it, out of faith for faith ...*

EVANGEL simply means *good news*, and we must look at the context to know what specific good news Paul is referring to. Here in Romans 1 we learn that the evangel is God's power for salvation *for everyone who is believing*.

The focus of the evangel is on God and His power. This power for salvation is *revealed* to those who are believing. Those who do not, or cannot believe, do not recognize God's power; at least not yet.

We also learn that in the evangel *God's righteousness is being revealed, out of faith for faith*. Out of whose faith? And for whose faith? Romans 3:22 sheds light: *A righteousness of God through Jesus Christ's faith, for all, and on all who are believing.*

So God's righteousness is brought forth out of Jesus Christ's faith, and it is ON all who are believing. [More on this when we look at 3:22]

Milestones in Paul's Ministry *(The Pause)*

> Trail Marker #10
>
> ## Is it our CHOICE to believe?

Consider this. Was it Abraham's choice to believe, or was the ability to believe granted to him by God in order that God's purposes might be fulfilled thru Abraham?

Did God speak equally to all men, giving all the same chance, but only Abraham believed? Or did God speak to Abraham in a way that he had not spoken to others, because Abraham was chosen by God? Think about these passages:

For you it is graciously granted, for Christ's sake, not only to be believing on Him ... (Philippians 1:29).

[Lydia] *whose heart the Lord opens up to heed what is spoken by Paul* (Acts 6:14).

The god of this eon blinds the apprehensions of the unbelieving so that the illumination of the evangel of the glory of Christ, Who is the Image of the invisible God, does not irradiate them (2 Corinthians 4:3).

Consider Paul's conversion. He did not simply *choose* to believe and become a follower of Christ. As a matter of fact Paul was the premier opponent of Christ. Yet he was chosen outside of his own "free will." Paul was directly spoken to in a way that others had not been spoken to, because he was the one chosen for this special commission.

So it would seem that the saints at Rome, the called of Jesus Christ, were those chosen by God and given the eyes to see and believe in order that God's purposes might be fulfilled thru them.

Milestones in Paul's Ministry *(The Pause)*

++ Some observations along the way ++

While God's righteousness is being revealed in the evangel, we also see the crucial *need* for the evangel; because God's indignation is revealed upon *mankind's natural state* apart from the grace of God. Let's follow Paul's line of reasoning.

- ✓ God has revealed Himself to mankind in a way that should be apparent. (1:19)
- ✓ But man does not glorify God or thank Him. (1:21)
- ✓ So God causes man's reasoning to be vain. And while men think they are wise, they are made to be stupid. (1:21)
- ✓ Man continues to turn away from God, changing God's incorruptible nature into likenesses that are corruptible, like a human being or a creature. (1:23)
- ✓ God gives man over to his base, fleshly nature; to the lusts of his heart. (1:24)
- ✓ Man gives way to uncleanness, to dishonoring his body (1:24) and to dishonorable passions. (1:26)
- ✓ So man's mind is made to be disqualified, doing things that are not befitting or appropriate (1:28).

This, then, is the sorry, hopeless state of mankind, before the revealing of God's solution; a righteousness from God which is announced in the evangel.

We can clearly see in this description of mankind the desperate need for a righteousness from God, as there is certainly no righteousness to be found within natural man.

Milestones in Paul's Ministry *(The Pause)*

> Trail Marker #11
> ## My evangel (2:16)

Paul uses a phrase in 2:16 that is very interesting: MY EVANGEL. We see this several times in Paul's writings. *My evangel* is the good news brought by Paul.

We must remember there is not just a single *gospel* or *evangel* in the Scriptures; but each time the word is used we must examine the context to determine what good news is being referred to. The fact that Paul uses the term *my evangel* instead of *the* evangel should cause us to ask what is unique about the evangel that he brings!

Paul was given revelation directly from Jesus Christ. *For neither did I accept it from a man, nor was I taught it, but it came through a revelation of Jesus Christ* (Galatians 1:12).

When Paul was converted, if he was commissioned to deliver the same evangel as the Twelve would it not have made sense for Paul to study under the Twelve who were eyewitnesses of all that Jesus said and did during His earthly ministry? Instead Christ revealed things directly to Paul. This is why Paul can refer to the news he brings as *my evangel*. And if we read the Scriptures carefully we will see that Paul's gospel is different from Peter's.

Trail Marker #12
None are just (3:10)

Not one is just – not even one.
Not one is understanding.
Not one is seeking out God
(3:10 ... from Psalm 14:1-3).

Since no one seeks out God on his own, how can *any* ever come to know God and be saved? How can any <u>believe</u> God if none are seeking Him?

Could it be that God <u>enables</u> some (the called) to believe, even when they were not seeking (as in the case of Paul), so that through this group all mankind will ultimately be blessed?

> ### Trail Marker #13
> ## God's righteousness revealed (3:21)

Yet now, apart from law, a righteousness of God is manifest; a righteousness of God through Jesus Christ's faith ...

This is not righteousness resulting from man's faith. It speaks of God's righteousness, manifest to mankind through <u>Jesus Christ's faith</u>.

... for all, and on all who are believing, for there is no distinction, for all sinned and are wanting of the glory of God.

God's righteousness is provided to mankind thru Jesus Christ's faith. Its effects are <u>for all</u>, because there is no distinction; all sinned and are wanting of the glory of God.

The <u>means</u> or <u>channel</u> thru which man receives this righteousness from God in this present age is thru faith, or belief. God's righteousness is for all, and it is currently received by those who are believing.

But there will come a day when Christ reveals Himself by sight to those unable to believe by faith; as in the case of Thomas (John 20:29).

Remember: God is the Saviour of all mankind, especially of believers (1 Timothy 4:11). Blessed are they who believe without seeing. In this way believers are *especial*. But as in Adam all died, so also in Christ will all be vivified.

Trail Marker #14
Belief reckoned as righteousness (4:2)

If Abraham was justified by acts he would have something to boast in. Abraham believes God, and it is reckoned to him for righteousness. To him who is not working yet is believing on Him Who is justifying the irreverent, his faith is reckoned for righteousness.

Abraham (from Genesis 15:6) is presented as an example. He was RECKONED righteous. He did not WORK for righteousness, thereby earning wages that were owed to him. He simply believed (apart from works), and this belief (same word in the Greek as faith) is reckoned by God as righteousness.

Abraham believed God when God promised he would become a father of many nations (Genesis 17:5) even though the promise seemed to be beyond expectation. This faith invigorated Abraham. And his belief is reckoned for righteousness.

So God spoke to Abraham, making a promise that was beyond belief, yet Abraham believed; and it was reckoned to him as righteousness.

Again I ask; did this belief come from within Abraham himself, or was the ability to comprehend God's promise and believe a gift from God? Remember the state of mankind apart from the grace of God. None are just. None are seeking out God.

Another consideration ... When God spoke to Abraham, he believed what God told him. What is it we are to believe today? Many churches maintain a list of what one must believe to be considered a believer.

Milestones in Paul's Ministry *(The Pause)*

> Trail Marker #15
> # Adam and Christ (5:12)

Even as through one man sin entered into the world, and through sin death, and thus death passed through into all mankind, on which all sinned.

Observe closely the parallel.

If, by the offense of the one, the many died, much rather the grace of God and the gratuity in grace, which is of the One Man, Jesus Christ, to the many superabounds. The judgment is out of one into condemnation, yet the grace is out of many offenses into a just award.

If, by the offense of the one, death reigns through the one, much rather, those obtaining the superabundance of grace and the gratuity of righteousness shall be reigning in life through the One, Jesus Christ.

Think about this. If Adam's one offense gave just the *opportunity* to sin, so that some become sinners while others not, then we could say that Christ's work brings justification only to *some*, conditioned upon man's acceptance.

But we note that man has no choice as to becoming a sinner. All have sinned. In this parallel then, <u>thus also</u> is the case with ultimate salvation. It is not conditioned on man's acceptance. Belief is the means for man's receiving God's righteousness in this present age, but ultimately all will see, all will be subjected to God, every knee will bow. Ultimately ALL will be justified thru Christ's death.

As it was through one offense for <u>all mankind</u> for condemnation, thus also it is through one just award for <u>all mankind</u> for life's justifying. For even as, through the disobedience of the one man, the many were constituted sinners, thus also, through the obedience of the One, the many shall be constituted just. (5:18)

Note that *the many* is a direct parallel to *all mankind*. *The many* is therefore used to symbolize *the all*. And note the global nature of these statements.

Certainly all mankind is condemned as a consequence of Adam's offense. None make a choice to be included in this group, and nothing can be done thru man's will to be excluded. In the parallel, then, the same is true of all mankind who are justified thru Christ's obedience!

A side note: We do not inherit Adam's sin. We inherit Adam's dying condition (mortality). Because of Adam's sin, death entered the world, and it was death that was then passed to all mankind. Death (mortality) in all mankind then led to sin by all mankind (the weakness of this flesh).

At birth we inherit death. Because we have inherited this death condition (mortality), we sin. None are righteous!

Milestones in Paul's Ministry *(The Pause)*

> **Trail Marker #16**
>
> ## If grace increases when we sin ... (6:1)

But if grace increases when we sin, should we not just continue sinning? May it not be coming to that! Those who are baptized into Christ Jesus are baptized into His death; so if we have died to sin how shall we still be living in sin?

And as Christ was roused from among the dead, so also we should be walking in newness of life. As we were crucified with Him that the body of Sin may be nullified, justifying us, we are not to be slaving for Sin as we once did.

Just as God *reckons* us righteous, even when our behaviors are not always righteous; so also we are instructed to *reckon* our old selves to be dead; even though our fleshly bodies may still be alive. Remember, when God spoke to Abraham He called that which was not as if it were.

Let not Sin, then, be reigning in your mortal body, for you to be obeying its lusts. Nor yet be presenting your members, as implements of injustice, to Sin, but present yourselves to God as if alive from among the dead, and your members as implements of righteousness to God. (6:12)

But since we are not under law, is it permissible to sin? May it not be coming to that! We are slaves to whoever we obey; Sin (for death), or Obedience (for righteousness). Now, being freed from Sin, you are enslaved to Righteousness.

This is stated as a fact! We who believe are freed from Sin, and we are now slaves to Righteousness. But while this is a fact, we make choices as we live that cause us to either be in harmony with our Master or in opposition to Him. It is not "anything goes" but behaving worthily, in accord with and in harmony with life choices God has revealed as acceptable in His eyes.

Trail Marker #17
The struggle (7:14)

The law is spiritual, yet I am fleshly.

The problem is not the law, but man. Without God's grace coming to the rescue, man faces a hopeless struggle as he seeks to gain righteousness thru the law.

For it is not the good that I will that I am doing, but the evil that I am not willing, this I am putting into practice. It is no longer I who am affecting it, but Sin which is making its home in me.

Good is not making its home in my flesh. It is not the good that I will that I am doing, but the evil that I am not willing; this I put into practice.

The struggle exists because of a friction between spirit and flesh.

A wretched man am I! What will rescue me out of this body of death?

Grace.

Most English Bible translations appear to leave the question in 7:24 unanswered. The Concordant Version provides the response: Grace!

Some ancient manuscripts omit the word grace, thereby leaving the question unanswered. But evidence seems to support those manuscripts which contain the response. Grace is what will rescue man in his hopeless state. Grace fits with Paul's line of thought throughout Romans, providing evidence that the manuscripts that include this response are the correct ones.

Trail Marker #18
In spirit (8:9)

Yet you are not in flesh, but in spirit, if so be that God's spirit is making its home in you. Now if anyone has not Christ's spirit, this one is not His. Now if Christ is in you, the body, indeed, is dead because of sin, yet the spirit is life because of righteousness.

Now we remember back to Romans 5:5, before any discussion of behavior took place, Paul told ALL of the believers ... *the love of God has been poured out in our hearts through the holy spirit which is being given to us.*

It is a FACT, not dependent upon man's response, that those who believe have been given the holy spirit. Therefore it is a matter of fact that ALL who believe are not in flesh, but in spirit; because God's spirit is making its home in them (8:9).

Paul admonishes the believer to present himself to God and to walk worthily; but he does not threaten a loss of position in Christ for those that are not exhibiting proper fruit. The solution to man's dilemma is 100% God, given to man freely thru His grace.

Despite how we may appear in the flesh, God has justified us in Christ. And the future judgment has been delegated to Christ, the very One Who died for us and Who pleads for us at God's right hand.

> ### Trail Marker #19
> ### Israel not permanently discarded (11:11)

Thru Israel's offense the nations find salvation, provoking jealousy in Israel. And if their casting away is the conciliation of the world, what will the taking back be if not life from among the dead?

Callousness, in part, on Israel has come until the complement of the nations may be entering. And thus all Israel shall be saved ... (11:25)

So Israel's casting away is not permanent, but only UNTIL the complement of the nations enters the ecclesia (called-out-ones). And the temporary casting-away of Israel serves a grand purpose; salvation to the nations.

There is stubbornness; and then mercy. Even this stubbornness in man is used by God for the good of mankind.

For God locks up all together in stubbornness, that He should be merciful to all. (11:30)

> Trail Marker #20
>
> ## How then shall we live? (12:1)

Present your bodies a sacrifice, living, holy, well pleasing to God, your logical divine service, and not to be configured to this eon, but to be transformed by the renewing of your mind, for you to be testing what is the will of God, good and well pleasing and mature.

Paul speaks of the appropriate conduct for believers. "I am entreating you, then" links Paul's discussion on behavior to that which he has previously said. It is as if he is saying, "In light of what God has done, live like this."

Note the language; I am ENTREATING you. Grace does not threaten or punish. It can only entreat.

Milestones in Paul's Ministry *(The Pause)*

> Trail Marker #21
> ## Bear with those weaker in faith (14:1)

Be taking to yourselves the infirm in the faith, but not for discrimination of reasonings.

As we deal with those who may have lesser faith than ourselves, we are to <u>receive</u> the infirm in faith; but not for *discrimination of reasonings*. In other words, we bear with those weaker in faith, but we do not look to them for an understanding of spiritual things.

One is believing to eat all things, yet the infirm one is eating greens. Let not him who is eating be scorning him who is not eating. Yet let not him who is not eating be judging him who is eating. Who are you who are judging another's domestic? To his own Master is he standing or falling.

One is deciding for one day rather than another day, yet one is deciding for every day. Let each one be fully assured in his own mind. He who is disposed to the day is disposed to it to the Lord.

The strong in faith are not to judge the weak in faith; and the weak in faith should not judge those who are stronger in faith (concerning, for example, eating different foods or observing different days). We do not judge a brother on these issues, as each is responsible only to His Master. It is a matter of conscience; Let each one be fully assured in his own mind (14:5). Each of us is guided by our conscience, with the help of the holy spirit that has been given to us. We take responsibility for ourselves, as opposed to judging others.

Relative to deciding for one day rather than another day (14:5); we observe that the Sabbath was never given as a command to the Gentiles. It was a part of the Law given to the Israelites. To keep the Sabbath as an observance of God's Law is to put ones-self under the Law. Furthermore, there is nowhere in Scripture a reference to a Sunday Sabbath for Christians! This is based purely on the traditions of men and not the Word of God. It is not wrong for a Believer to set aside Sunday, or any other day, to the Lord, if he chooses to do so. But God's Word should not be distorted in calling for any required observances on any particular day. Such mandatory observances

Milestones in Paul's Ministry *(The Pause)*

---

may have been required for Israel in times past, but never for the Body of Christ in this present age. To enforce a Sabbath day or any other portion of the Law would be to reject Christ (see Galatians).

> ### Trail Marker #22
> ### Place no stumbling block (14:13)

Decide this, not to place a stumbling block for a brother, or a snare.

As we exercise the measure of faith given to us, a major consideration must be the possibility of causing others to stumble. That which is right or wrong is determined by our individual conscience; but we are not to place stumbling blocks before others.

Nothing is contaminating of itself, except that the one reckoning anything to be contaminating, to that one it is contaminating. If because of food your brother is sorrowing, you are no longer walking according to love. Consequently we are pursuing that which makes for peace and that which edifies others.

It is ideal not to be eating meat, nor to be drinking wine, nor to do anything by which your brother is stumbling or is being snared or weakened.

1 Corinthians

Trail Marker #23
No schisms (1:10)

I am entreating you that all may be saying the same thing, and there may be no schisms among you, but you may be attuned to the same mind and to the same opinion. There are strifes among you. Some are saying "I am of Paul," and others "I am of Apollos" or "I am of Cephas" or "I am of Christ."

Strife had entered the ecclesia, much like denominational differences and the differences between individual churches today. Paul entreats the ecclesia to all be saying the same thing, with no schisms, attuned to the same mind and to the same opinion.

Truth is truth, and once one understands truth he will be attuned to all others who see truth. All will be of the same mind; the mind of Christ.

But schism is not eliminated by simply consenting, without debate, to the loudest voices in the ecclesia. We should not be lobbying for our opinions as to the things of God. All within the ecclesia, the Body of Christ, should be seeking, and working together to understand the mind of God as revealed in His word.

Remember that in Paul's day there was not a Baptist Church, a Methodist Church, etc. There was simply one ecclesia. They met together in smaller groups, or ecclesias, often in peoples' homes, and likely very informally, but all were a part of the single ecclesia. How complicated and divided the ecclesia has become in our present world of denominations, independent churches, articles of religion, membership covenants, rituals and ceremonies. How the ecclesia has been systematized, fragmented and split apart; far from the unity Paul called for.

> ### Trail Marker #24
> ### Not to be baptizing (1:13)

You were not baptized into the name of Paul. I thank God that I baptize none of you except Crispus and Gaius and the household of Stephanas. Christ does not commission me to be baptizing, but to bring the evangel.

Paul's commission is to bring the evangel; not to baptize. Notice how unimportant baptism seems to be from Paul's perspective.

But what about "The Great Commission" found in Matthew? *"Going, then, disciple all the nations, baptizing them ..."* (Matthew 28:19).

While most believers in the church today see "The Great Commission" as *their* commission, obviously Paul does not. He is not commissioned to be baptizing.

"The Great Commission" is taken out of context today. It speaks of Israel discipling the nations, as will be done in the end times upon the earth (Revelation). It does not speak to the church today at all. We have a different commission; not the one found in Matthew 28.

Milestones in Paul's Ministry *(The Pause)*

> Trail Marker #25
> ## Maturity is needed (3:1)

But you are still fleshly. I could not speak to you as to spiritual things, but only as to fleshly things.

Despite the fact that God has revealed things, and that believers have the holy spirit and should be able to understand, they were minors in Christ and could not understand spiritual things. How does Paul discern that these believers are fleshly, and unable to understand spiritual things?

Where there is jealousy and strife among you, are you not fleshly and walking according to man? For whenever anyone may be saying, "I am of Paul" or "I am of Apollos" is he not fleshly?

Division is the manifestation of man's walking according to the flesh. Men were being elevated and followed, creating divisions much like those seen in the Church today; I follow the Methodists; I follow the Baptists, etc.

++

Another very significant observation ... Based on what Paul is saying here, we should not expect the more advanced truths that he would share with the mature, which we find in his later "perfection epistles" (Ephesians, Colossians, Philippians).

Trail Marker #26
Building on the one foundation (3:10)

If anyone is building on this foundation gold and silver, precious stones, wood, grass, straw, each one's work will become apparent, for the day will make it evident, for it is being revealed by fire.

And the fire will be testing each one's work; what kind it is. If anyone's work is remaining which he builds on it, he will get wages. If anyone's work is burned up, he will forfeit it, yet he shall be saved, yet as through fire (3:13).

The works of a believer will be evaluated by God at some future time (Romans 14:12; 2 Corinthians 5:10). We note that the absence of good works does not jeopardize one's salvation, but it will affect the wages (rewards) received.

Trail Marker #27
Dealing with immoral behavior (5:1)

There is prostitution among you, and such prostitution which is not even named among the nations, so that someone has his father's wife. And you do not mourn but are puffed up.

So are we to judge ... or not? Paul has warned against judging. But here he says there is a place for judging within the ecclesia, at least concerning immoral behavior. Rather than mourning the immoral behavior in their midst, the ecclesia is "puffed up;" apparently having justified the behavior thru reason.

Remove the one committing this act. Give up such a one to Satan for the extermination of the flesh, that the spirit may be saved in the day of the Lord Jesus.

Observe that discipline of the immoral brother is not vindictive, but toward the goal of his salvation. Correction is brought to the Body of Christ, and the welfare of the individual being disciplined is considered. This expresses God's heart; that none are punished endlessly, and that correction is accomplished.

Are you not aware that a little leaven is leavening the whole kneading? Clean out, then, the old leaven.

Addressing matters of immorality within the ecclesia also serves to preserve the ecclesia itself.

Do not be commingling with paramours. It is not as to the paramours of this world, or the greedy and extortionate, or idolaters, else you ought to come out of the world. Yet now I write to you not to be commingling with anyone named a brother, if he should be a paramour, or greedy, or an idolater, or a reviler, or a drunkard, or an extortioner. With such a one you are not even to be eating.

What is it to me to be judging those outside? You are not judging those within! God is judging those outside. Expel the wicked one from among yourselves.

Trail Marker #28
Giving up rights (9:1)

Am I not free? Am I not an apostle? Have only I and Barnabas no right not to be working? Who is warring and supplying his own rations? The Lord prescribes that those who are announcing the evangel are to be living of the evangel.

As an apostle Paul could have insisted upon certain rights. But he forfeited rights for the sake of the evangel.

Nevertheless we do not use this right. We are forgoing all, lest we may be giving any hindrance to the evangel of Christ.

Paul was entrusted with an administration; bringing the evangel. He will not let anything stand in the way of that commission, even if it required him to forfeit certain rights and freedoms.

I enslave myself to all, that I should be gaining the more. To the Jews I became as a Jew. To those under law I became as under law, to be gaining those under law. To all have I become all; that I should undoubtedly be saving some.

All is permitted, but not all is edifying. Let one not seek his own welfare, but the welfare of another.

Why is my freedom being decided by another's conscience? Whether you are eating or drinking, or anything you are doing, do all for the glory of God. And become not a stumbling block. I seek not my own expedience but that of the many, that they may be saved.

> ### Trail Marker #29
> ### Assembling not for the better (11:17)

You are coming together, not for the better. I am hearing of schisms.

Something to keep in mind when the Body of Christ assembles. Assembling for the sake of assembling is not necessarily a good thing. It is possible to come together, but not for the better.

Milestones in Paul's Ministry *(The Pause)*

> ### Trail Marker #30
> ## You are the Body of Christ (12:12)

The body is not one member, but many; yet all the members are one body. In one spirit we all are baptized into one body, whether Jews or Greeks, slaves or free. Not all are an ear or an eye. If the whole body were an eye, where would be the hearing? God places the members in the body as He wills.

The eye cannot say to the hand, I have no need of you.

And when one member is suffering, all the members are sympathizing. When one member is being esteemed, all the members are rejoicing with it.

God placed in the ecclesia; first apostles, second, prophets, third, teachers, thereupon powers, thereupon graces of healing, supports, pilotage (steering/governing), *species of languages. Not all members are the same. Not all are apostles. Not all are prophets. Yet be zealous for the greater graces.*

Compare the list of spiritual gifts found here with the list in Paul's later revelation in Ephesians 4:11. Could the difference be accounted to Paul's statement in 12:31; "a path suited to transcendence?" In the later list, some of the "lesser" gifts (powers, healing, languages) are omitted. The termination of some gifts was foretold in 13:8.

Are some of these gifts now extinct?

Remember that Paul could not share deeper spiritual truths with the Corinthians as they were not mature (3:1). Yet he was able to share these secrets with the more mature believers (Ephesians 4:13; Philippians 3:14; Colossians 1:28; Colossians 4:12).

Furthermore, Paul "completed" the Word of God as noted in Colossians 1:25; so there would appear to be no longer a need for prophecy to provide a word from God. Miracles and healings were manifestations that accompanied the kingdom evangel, as signs of what was to come when the kingdom came upon the earth. But the expectation of the Body of Christ is not upon the earth. We do not look for Christ to come to reign upon His throne in Jerusalem; that is Israel's expectation. We listen for the trumpet to sound, and for Christ to snatch us away and meet us in the air, to take us to be with Him in the celestials (1 Thessalonians 4:13ff).

Could it be that by the time Paul wrote to the Ephesians, some of the gifts had ceased; accounting for their absence from the Ephesians list?

Prophecies will be discarded, languages will cease, knowledge will be discarded; but love is never lapsing. Out of an instalment we know and are prophesying. When maturity may be coming, that which is out of an installment shall be discarded. (1 Corinthians 13:8)

Milestones in Paul's Ministry *(The Pause)*

> Trail Marker #31
>
> ## The consummation (15:21)

Since, in fact, through a man came death, through a man, also, comes the resurrection of the dead. For even as, in Adam, all are dying, thus also, in Christ, shall all be vivified.

Consider the direct one-for-one, all-for-all parallel between Adam and Christ!

Yet each in his own class ...
  The Firstfruit, Christ;
  Thereupon those who are Christ's in His presence;
  Thereafter the consummation.

Here we see the order of the resurrection. First Christ; second those who are Christ's (believers); and third the consummation. Paul now describes this final stage of the resurrection; the consummation ...

Whenever He (Christ) may be giving up the kingdom to His God and Father, whenever He should be nullifying all sovereignty and all authority and power. For He must be reigning until He should be placing all His enemies under His feet. The last enemy being abolished is death. For He subjects all under His feet. Whenever all may be subjected to Him, then the Son Himself also shall be subjected to (God); that God may be All in all.

THIS IS THE CLIMAX OF THE SCRIPTURES AND OF THE ENTIRE HISTORY OF MANKIND!

As Paul speaks of the consummation he speaks of things not revealed by God through those who proclaimed the kingdom evangel; not even John when he penned that which Christ revealed to him in the book of Revelation.

For any who might conclude that Revelation is the latest revelation from God as to His plans for future times, consider the following:

In Revelation 22:5 we read of His slaves who are reigning, and in Revelation 21:24 we read of kings of the earth. But in 1 Corinthians 15:24 we are told of a time when all sovereignty, authority and power are nullified.

In Revelation 21:5 we see Christ seated on the throne. But in 1 Corinthians 15:28 we read that Christ will reign UNTIL all enemies are under His feet, at which time He Himself becomes subject to God the Father.

In Revelation 21:8 we read that the lake of fire is in operation, and it is referred to as the "second death." But in 1 Corinthians 15:27 we read that the last enemy, death, is abolished.

In Revelation 22:2 we read of leaves on the tree which are for the "cure" of the nations. This implies bodies that are in need of the leaves to sustain health. But in 1 Corinthians 15:42-44 we read of an incorruptible body.

In Revelation 21:12,14,24 we read of the twelve tribes, the twelve apostles (which would not include Paul) and the nations outside the city, respectively. But in Galatians 3:28 Paul speaks of no distinction between Jew or Greek; and we see no distinction anywhere in 1 Corinthians 15.

Revelation has a distinct Jewish character. It is a continuation of the kingdom evangel to the sheep of Israel, after the Body of Christ has been removed from the earth (1 Thessalonians 4:13). Revelation speaks of a physical realm when the kingdom comes upon the earth; much like our present world but with Christ reigning and keeping evil in check. But 1 Corinthians 15 is very obviously referring to a spiritual realm, with no corruption, reign or power. All are subjected. There are no enemies, no death, no sin, no rebellion. The purpose of the eons has been achieved, and God is now All in all.

Revelation speaks of the final age (eon) upon the earth. 1 Corinthians 15 (the consummation) speaks of a time after the ages have concluded; when God's purpose of the eons (Ephesians 3:11) has been accomplished.

Flesh and blood is not able to enjoy an allotment in the kingdom of God, neither is corruption enjoying the allotment of incorruption.

An incorruptible body will be needed in the celestial kingdom.

A secret to you am I telling! We all, indeed, shall not be put to repose, yet we shall be changed, in an instant, in the twinkle of an eye, at the last trump. For He will be trumpeting, and the dead will be roused incorruptible, and we shall be changed. For this corruptible must put on incorruption, and this mortal put on immortality.

2 Corinthians

> ### Trail Marker #32
> ### The evangel is "covered" (4:3)

If our evangel is covered, it is covered in those who are perishing. The god of this eon blinds the apprehensions of the unbelieving so that the illumination of the evangel of the glory of Christ, Who is the Image of the invisible God, does not irradiate them.

If unbelievers are blinded by *the god of this eon*. How can they ever come to believe?

All of mankind would be blinded had God not chosen to reveal and enlighten the ecclesia (called-out-ones). With the god of this eon blinding the apprehensions of man, who can believe except those God has called and enlightened?

Note the sequence. It is not that unbelievers fail to believe and are thereby blinded and perishing. Instead, they are blinded by the god of this eon and therefore do not believe.

With the god of this eon blinding mankind, who CAN believe? God, in His grace and wisdom, breaks thru the power of the god of this eon and <u>enables some to believe</u>; in order that the evangel is proclaimed thru these believers; leading to the ultimate goal ... ALL mankind is ultimately blessed.

> ### Trail Marker #33
> ### In the body or with the Lord? (5:1)

We are groaning and are burdened; not wanting to be stripped and found naked, but to be dressed in our habitation that is out of heaven, that the mortal may be swallowed up by life. God gives us the earnest of the spirit.

Being at home in the body, we are away from home from the Lord (for by faith are we walking, not by perception), yet we are encouraged and are delighting rather to be away from home out of the body and to be at home with the Lord.

When a believer dies, does he go immediately to heaven?

This passage is often used to support the thinking that upon death the believer immediately goes to heaven. Note, though, that Paul mentions three states;

- ✓ In the body,
- ✓ At home with the Lord, and
- ✓ Naked/stripped/undressed (5:4).

Paul is in the body and he longs to be with the Lord, and as he writes to the Corinthians he is thinking the time is short before the resurrection occurs. But until the resurrection those who have died are "naked," or without a body.

The Scriptures reveal that upon death, we sleep in hades (unseen state) with no consciousness until the Lord calls and we are resurrected.

> ## Trail Marker #34
> ## Not acquainted according to flesh (5:14)

The love of Christ is constraining us. If One died for the sake of all, consequently all died. And He died for the sake of all that those who are living should by no means still be living to themselves, but to the One dying and being roused for their sakes.

So that we, from now on, are acquainted with no one according to flesh. Yet even if we have known Christ according to flesh, nevertheless now we know Him so no longer.

Even Christ is no longer known "according to flesh," yet most in the church today look primarily to Christ's teachings according to flesh as found in the "kingdom evangel" He proclaimed during His earthly ministry (while in flesh); His message that the kingdom to be restored unto Israel was near, and repentance was required to enter.

Milestones in Paul's Ministry *(The Pause)*

> Trail Marker #35
>
> **A new creation** (5:17)

So that, if anyone is in Christ, there is a new creation: the primitive passed by. Lo! There has come new!

Are we to be <u>born again</u>? Or a <u>new creation</u>?

Israel was told they must be born again. The Body of Christ is not to be born again but is instead a new creation.

Trail Marker #36
God conciliated the world (5:18)

[God] conciliates us to Himself through Christ, and is giving us the dispensation of the conciliation, how that God was in Christ, conciliating the world to Himself, not reckoning their offenses to them, and placing in us the word of the conciliation.

God conciliated the world to Himself. Observe the one-sided nature of what God has done. Regardless of man's actions or beliefs, God was, in Christ, conciliating the world to Himself; not reckoning man's offenses to Him.

Upon believing and becoming conciliated to God on our part, we have a two-sided "reconciliation." But we see here that even with respect to unbelievers, God is conciliated and not reckoning, or counting, their offenses.

Through Christ's death we were <u>conciliated</u> to God. (Romans 5:10)

How different is this when compared with the kingdom evangel proclaimed by John the Baptist: *Repent. The kingdom is near. Flee the wrath that is to come.*

Milestones in Paul's Ministry *(The Pause)*

Trail Marker #37
Ambassadors (5:20)

For Christ, then, are we AMBASSADORS, as of God entreating through us. We are beseeching for Christ's sake, 'Be conciliated to God!' For the One not knowing sin, He makes to be a sin offering for our sakes that we may be becoming God's righteousness in Him.

This is THE GREAT COMMISSION to the Body of Christ! It is OUR commission in this present day.

The message given to Christ's ambassadors to proclaim is simply, *Be conciliated to God. God is conciliated to the world, not reckoning man's offenses against Him; therefore, Be conciliated to God.*

Today we hear a much different message proclaimed by most churches. The kingdom is being proclaimed, based upon Jesus' words in the four gospels. But that message pertained to Israel.

Today we often hear a mixture of law with grace. But that is the DIFFERENT gospel that Paul warns about in Galatians 1:7. And many of Christ's ambassadors today are concocting their own message or proclaiming a message from somewhere in Scripture that pertains to a different group of people.

As Christ's Ambassadors we must take care to proclaim the CORRECT message for this present era!

> ### Trail Marker #38
> ## Grace is sufficient (12:7)

Lest I should be lifted up by the transcendence of the revelations, there was given to me a splinter in the flesh, a messenger of Satan, that he may be buffeting me, lest I may be lifted up. For this I entreat the Lord thrice, that it should withdraw from me. And He has protested to me, 'Sufficient for you is My grace, for My power in infirmity is being perfected.'

Wherefore I delight in infirmities, in outrages, in necessities, in persecutions, in distress, for Christ's sake, for, whenever I may be weak, then I am powerful.

How different this is from the "name it and claim it" theology, or those purporting to have a miraculous healing ministry. Healings and miracles may have accompanied the proclamation of the kingdom evangel, for it pertained to earthly things; the kingdom to be restored upon the earth. But Paul's ministry pertains to the heavenly realm.

The Body of Christ has no expectation upon this earth. Grace is sufficient; there is no need for miracles. God's power is perfected in man's weakness.

Galatians

Milestones in Paul's Ministry *(The Pause)*

> Trail Marker #39
>
> ## To extricate us ... (1:4)

The Lord Jesus Christ gave Himself for our sins, so that He might extricate us out of the present wicked eon.

This reference to being *extricated out of the present wicked eon* appears to refer to the snatching away of the Body of Christ in 1 Thessalonians 4:13-18 (commonly referred to as the rapture), when Christ will descend and when the dead and the living will be snatched away to meet the Lord in the air.

Currently God is working thru the Body of Christ and not Israel. But after the snatching-away, when the Body is removed from the earth, the events described in the book of Revelation will take place upon the earth. And then once again God will be working thru Israel upon the earth, which explains the many references to Israel throughout the book of Revelation.

++

Eon comes from the Greek *aion* and refers to a period of time of indefinite length. We remember from our study of science that the word eon refers to a very long time period; but not endlessness.

We sometimes see aion (or eon) in Scripture in the singular, and sometimes in the plural. A careful study of Scripture reveals that there was a time before the eons (2 Timothy 1:9; Titus 1:2; 1 Corinthians 2:7) and there will be an end of the eons (1 Corinthians 10:11; Hebrews 9:26). There will be eons to come in the future (Matthew 12:32; Ephesians 1:21; Hebrews 6:5) and there will be an end to this present eon (Matthew 13:39; Matthew 24:3).

And there are a number of instances where Scripture refers to this present eon, as in this passage in Galatians 1.

Modern Bible translations confuse this distinction between the eons, using the word eternal where that word seems to fit, and using another word (like age or world) where eternal will not fit the context. But if we translate the Bible consistently we will see very clearly that there are different time periods being referred to (eons or ages), each with a beginning and an end.

> Trail Marker #40
> ## A different evangel (1:6)

I am marveling that swiftly you are transferred from that which calls you in the grace of Christ to a DIFFERENT evangel, which is not another, except it be that some who are disturbing you want also to DISTORT the evangel of Christ.

The Galatians were being led astray. The false message that is misleading them is not just another message of the same kind. It is a DIFFERENT message; a DISTORTION of the evangel of Christ. Paul warns that if anyone brings an evangel different from the one that he brings, it should be rejected.

If ever we also, or a messenger out of heaven, should be bringing an evangel to you beside that which we bring to you, let him be anathema!

Even if Peter, for example, were to bring an evangel different from what Paul had brought, it should be rejected.

As we read on, we will see that this is the problem. Peter and the Twelve were commissioned to proclaim an evangel to the Circumcision (Israel), while Paul has been called as a different kind of apostle (not one of the Twelve) and to declare a different evangel to the Body of Christ (thereby explaining the opposition Paul encounters). So Paul declares, "Listen only to the evangel that I bring."

But today most churches proclaim the evangel from Peter and the Twelve, ignoring Paul's admonition!

Many within the church today are being led astray to a different evangel; a distortion of the evangel; that mixes-in elements from the Circumcision evangel.

Most denominations trace their pastoral authority to Peter as the rock upon whom the church was originated. But the ecclesia (called-out-ones) when Christ spoke those words to Peter was exclusively Jewish; and in Paul God is working in a different way, through the Body of Christ comprised of Gentiles and Jews alike with no distinction.

We who are within the Body of Christ today should heed the strong words Paul has for those who are presenting a different, distorted evangel; as he implores those in Galatia to accept only the evangel that he brings.

> ### Trail Marker #41
> ### Paul's evangel came thru revelation (1:11)

If Paul was to proclaim the same message as the Twelve (but only to a different group of recipients; the Gentiles), it would have made sense to have Paul spend time being trained by the Twelve. After all, they were with Christ during the entire time of His ministry upon the earth. They witnessed His miracles, His crucifixion, His resurrection and His ascension into heaven. But Paul makes it clear that his evangel was not received from a man.

For I am making known to you, brethren, as to the evangel which is being brought by me, that it is not in accord with man. For neither did I accept it from a man, nor was I taught it, but it came through a revelation of Jesus Christ.

God severed Paul (1:15) to cut him apart from the others of his Jewish brethren. God called him through His grace, as opposed to judging him for his persecution of Christ. After his conversion, Paul did not seek guidance from Peter and the other apostles in Jerusalem. ...

I did not immediately submit it to flesh and blood, neither came I up to Jerusalem to those who were apostles before me, but I came away into Arabia, and I return again to Damascus.

It is significant that Paul distanced himself in this way from the other apostles. The evangel he proclaimed was not taught to him by the others; it was revealed to Him by Jesus Christ. This should cause us to ask why this direct revelation was necessary.

Could it be that the message Paul was to bear was different? Many Bible teachers today indiscriminately teach equally from Paul's writings and from the others as if there is no difference. But Paul goes out of his way to distance himself from the others here in Galatians.

By blending together Paul's evangel with the evangel proclaimed by Peter and the others of the Twelve, are we guilty of distorting the evangel intended for us; and are we being led astray by a different evangel?

Milestones in Paul's Ministry *(The Pause)*

> **Trail Marker #42**
> ## Two different evangels (2:7)

I have been entrusted with the evangel of the Uncircumcision, according as Peter of the Circumcision.

There were two different evangels (gospels) to be proclaimed to two different people groups. The evangels were different. Paul did not simply bear the same evangel as Peter, but to the Uncircumcision. He was entrusted with "the evangel of the Uncircumcision."

If Paul had consented to blending the two messages together, much controversy would have been eliminated. And when Paul returned to Jerusalem late in his ministry he would not have been opposed by the Jews who believed but who were zealous for the law (Acts 21:20).

But to blend the evangels together would have been a distortion and would have created a DIFFERENT evangel; and this is what Paul so vehemently defends against.

In Jerusalem, all agree that we, indeed, are to be for the nations, yet they for the Circumcision.

It seems clear that at this point in time there are two evangels; one proclaimed by Paul and Barnabas to the nations, and another by the Twelve to the Jews. Paul does not contend that Peter and the others needed to change the evangel they had been proclaiming to make it consistent with his. But they agreed to take the respective evangels entrusted to them to the groups God had placed under their care.

There appears, then, to be a Jewish ecclesia (church) hearing the evangel as proclaimed by Peter, and a Gentile ecclesia (church) hearing Paul's evangel. And if we study closely the writings of Paul as compared with the writings of Peter, James and John we will see many differences.

Evangel of Uncircumcision (Paul)	Evangel of Circumcision
The Body of Christ	The Bride of Christ
New creation	Born again
Expectation in the heavens	Expectation upon the earth
Awaiting Christ to snatch us away	Awaiting Christ to reign upon the earth
Justified by faith alone (Romans 4:1-3)	Justified by faith plus works (James 2:24)
No legal requirements (circumcision, sabbath, tithing, etc.)	Legal requirements observed

The confusion with there being two different evangels in this "transitional" period can be seen by Paul's comments regarding Peter's hypocrisy. (2:11)

If you, being inherently a Jew, are living as the nations, and not as the Jews, how are you compelling the nations to be judaizing?

Despite the agreement in Jerusalem, when Cephas (Peter) comes to Antioch he severed himself from those of the nations, because he feared those of the Circumcision.

This, then, is the problem that Paul was contending with in this letter. The Jews were adding to Paul's evangel by requiring the Gentiles to observe elements of the law. There is conflict between Paul (and the message he brings to the Gentiles) and the Jewish believers. And the two groups (Circumcision believers and Uncircumcision believers) are largely severed from one another.

The message proclaimed by Paul to the Gentiles is freedom apart from any elements from the law, and the Circumcision believers have difficulty accepting that God is doing something so different apart from the Jews who had been His chosen instrument in the past.

> Trail Marker #43
> ## Don't repudiate grace (2:21)

I am not repudiating the grace of God, for if righteousness is through law, consequently Christ died gratuitously.

Adding legal requirements is rejecting grace. If righteousness can be gained thru works of law, then Christ would have died for no purpose.

Those wanting to add requirements from the law (like circumcision) to become righteous are repudiating God's grace and nullifying what Christ has accomplished thru His death. The Galatians had been deceived and were repudiating grace to fall back on the law once again.

Are we not guilty of the same infraction today if we add requirements to pure and simple <u>belief</u>? Baptism, sabbath observance, acceptance of church membership vows, allegiance to the trinity doctrine, etc.?

> ### Trail Marker #44
> ### No Jew nor Greek (3:28)

There is no Jew nor yet Greek, there is no slave nor yet free, there is no male and female, for you all are one in Christ Jesus.

No Jew nor Greek? This is something new.

There are no fleshly distinctions. Always in the past, preference had been given to the Jew first. Not so now thru Paul's evangel. The nations are now enjoyers of the allotment ...

> Trail Marker #45
> ## Why turn back? (4:9)

Knowing God, yet rather being known by God, how are you turning back again to the infirm and poor elements for which you want to slave again anew? Days are you scrutinizing, and months and seasons and years.

Paul seems to be referring to a dependence upon recognizing certain days as was required by the law, and which sons of God had been freed from; sabbaths and required feast days.

For freedom Christ frees us! Stand firm, then, and be not again enthralled with the yoke of slavery. (5:1)

If you should be circumcising, Christ will benefit you nothing. Now I am attesting again to every man who is circumcising, that he is a debtor to do the whole law. Exempted from Christ were you who are being justified in law. You fall out of grace.

Milestones in Paul's Ministry *(The Pause)*

> ## Trail Marker #46
> ## Freedom is not a license ^(5:13)

You were called for freedom, brethren, only use not the freedom for an incentive to the flesh, but through love be slaving for one another.

Some still think there is a need for legal requirements. They are afraid to remove legal requirements from the gospel (sabbath, tithing, Sermon on the Mount requirements, drinking, smoking; the list goes on) because they fear that believers will live however they please, guided only by satisfying their fleshly desires.

But Paul does not respond to this challenge by adding legal requirements to his message of grace. The law has nothing to do with one's position with God.

But without adding legal requirements to his evangel, Paul does insist that our freedom is not to be abused.

The entire law is fulfilled in one word, in this: You shall love your associate as yourself.

Love fulfills the law. Living to the flesh is to have selfish motivations. Living by love is to have selfless motivations; to be guided by a concern for one's associate.

Walk in spirit, and you should under no circumstances be consummating the lust of the flesh.

Walking in the spirit (or not) has no bearing on our justification or our being reckoned righteous, which is dependent only upon belief (faith). But Paul admonishes the ecclesia to walk in spirit.

For the flesh is lusting against the spirit, yet the spirit against the flesh. Now these are opposing one another, lest you should be doing whatever you may want.

If the believer is not under the law, what prevents him from doing whatever he wants; using his freedom as a license to sin?

Milestones in Paul's Ministry *(The Pause)*

The holy spirit is given to the believer. When the believer allows himself to be led by the flesh, the opposition of the spirit is felt. If the spirit did not oppose the flesh through this inner struggle, we could be guided by the flesh with no reservations. But it is the struggle that holds us in check; the conscience.

Now, if you are led by spirit, you are not still under law.

Those who walk in spirit fulfill the demands of the law without compulsion. The spirit of the law is fulfilled without any need for its form. They are <u>led</u> by the spirit and are not under law.

It is a <u>fact</u> that the believer is led by spirit and is therefore not under law. In response, Paul prompts the ecclesia to walk in spirit.

> **Trail Marker #47**
> ## Specially ... (6:10)

Consequently, then, as we have occasion, we are working for the good of all, yet <u>specially</u> for the family of faith.

Believers may be under persecution and may be in need of works of goodness from others even more so than non-believers. But we work for the good of all, not just fellow believers.

Specially in this passage comes from the Greek *malista*. We see in this context that we are to work not exclusively for the good of believers. We are to work for the good of ALL; in a *special* way for believers, but for the good of all.

The same Greek word is found in 1 Timothy 4:10 where we read that God is the Saviour of all mankind, *especially* of believers. Most within the church today would say that God will save only those who believe in this lifetime, but this passage tells us that God is the Saviour of *all*. Salvation pertains to the believer in a SPECIAL way, for he enjoys the expectation thru faith, and will have a special function in the age to come.

But God is not the Saviour exclusively of believers; He is the Saviour of all.

Milestones in Paul's Ministry *(The Pause)*

> Trail Marker #48
>
> ## Correct doctrine is important

Galatians is a very important letter, largely ignored by the church today!

Many in the church indiscriminately mix the evangel of Paul with the evangel of Peter and the Twelve, which was intended for the Jewish ecclesia (called-out-ones) who looked for the restoration of the kingdom upon the earth. Many impose requirements upon the believer; water baptism, tithing, church attendance, church membership, consenting to a list of doctrinal beliefs based on the church's interpretation of Scripture.

Paul vehemently opposed any additions to the justification and righteousness gratuitously given by God, through Christ Jesus. He warned against anyone preaching an evangel different from the one he preached; yet today's pulpits proclaim a different evangel (the Circumcision evangel) instead of Paul's evangel.

Observe the importance of correct doctrine!

When others attempt to teach the need for elements of the law to be added to the gospel, Paul does not dodge the issue. Nor does he compromise for the sake of unity and love.

Love is the most important thing (1 Corinthians 14), but doctrine is also important. Whereas the two letters to the Corinthians were concerned more with practical matters, Galatians is focused on addressing doctrinal error.

"If ever we also, or a messenger out of heaven, should be bringing an evangel to you <u>beside that which we bring to you</u>, let him be anathema!

<u>Ephesians</u>

> Trail Marker #49
> ## Spiritual blessings (1:3)

Blessed be the God and Father of our Lord Jesus Christ, Who blesses us with every spiritual blessing among the celestials, in Christ.

These are not, then, blessings realized in the flesh upon this earth as was the case with Israel, but spiritual blessings among the celestials, or heavenly realms.

The believer today is not promised fleshly blessings ... but spiritual blessings.

> ### Trail Marker #50
> ### The secret (1:9)

Making known to us the secret of His will (in accord with His delight, which He purposed in Him) to have an administration of the complement of the eras, to head up all in the Christ – both that in the heavens and that on the earth.

God revealed to Paul a SECRET that had been concealed in the past. Therefore Paul's evangel was most certainly DIFFERENT from the evangel proclaimed by Peter and others of the Circumcision.

God chose us, a subset of humanity, to make known a secret.

The Greek *musterion* is clearly not a "mystery" in the sense that it is something we can solve or figure out. It is a SECRET that was CONCEALED in the past and is now made known by God.

And the secret is this. As a complement to the eras ... the history of mankind that has preceded and that is a display of man's wickedness, sinfulness and imperfection ... God now reveals His plan to head up all in Christ, not only that which is in the heavens but also that which is on the earth.

Despite the chaos, wickedness and destruction we see all around us in this world, God's secret is that He is in the process of solving all of this.

A complement is something that brings completion. There is one part, and by adding a complement that part is made whole, or complete. The chaos in the world today is in the process of being made whole or complete by the *complement* that God has provided. All, not just some but all, will be headed up by Christ. (Turn to 1 Corinthians 15:20-28 to see this taking place.)

> Trail Marker #51
> ## All in accord with the counsel of His will (1:11)

God is operating all in accord with the counsel of His will, that we should be for the laud of His glory, who are pre-expectant in the Christ.

If this is so, what can possibly prevent Christ from heading up all that is in the heavens and upon the earth?

Furthermore,

If God is the Saviour of all mankind, especially (though not exclusively) of believers, (1 Timothy 4:10), and

If it is God's will or desire that all mankind be saved and come into a realization of the truth, (1 Timothy 2:4), and

If God is operating all in accord with the counsel of His will, (Ephesians 1:12),

Then what can possibly prevent these things from taking place?

++

Pre-expectant? This is an interesting phrase at the end of 1:12. *Pre-expectant* implies that what we, the saints, enjoy (sonship, forgiveness, grace) is just step one. All of humanity is *expectant* of these things, for God is in the process of heading up all in Christ. We who have been chosen beforehand, to serve God's purpose in some way, are *pre-expectant*.

Milestones in Paul's Ministry *(The Pause)*

> ### Trail Marker #52
> ## Coming to a realization of God (1:17)

That God may be giving you a spirit of wisdom and revelation in the <u>realization of Him</u>, the eyes of your heart having been enlightened,

For you <u>to perceive</u> what is the expectation of His calling,

And what the riches of the glory of the enjoyment of His allotment among the saints,

And what the transcendent greatness of His power for us who are believing,

Which is operative in the Christ, raising Him from among the dead and seating Him at His right hand among the celestials, up over every sovereignty and authority and power and lordship.

God had demonstrated His power in rousing Christ from among the dead and seating Him among the celestials (the heavens) with a position above all of creation.

But the believers were not yet *enlightened*; they did not yet *realize* what they could expect in terms of their allotment, or the glory of what they could expect in the future.

It is this failure to fully understand their expectation that would seem to give cause to Paul to write this letter. Whereas Romans provides basic doctrine, Ephesians goes beyond that (as a graduate course) and provides more advanced doctrine intended to further enlighten the believers.

> ### Trail Marker #53
> ## Purpose of the ecclesia – the complement (1:22)

He subjects all under Christ's feet, and gives Him, as Head over all, to the ecclesia which is His body, <u>the complement</u> by which all in all is being completed.

We see here that God subjects all under Christ (1:22) and Christ is the One completing the all in all (1:23). We see this process being completed in 1 Corinthians 28 when God does, in fact, become all in all.

But we also see in this passage an amazing fact that tells us, at least in part, why God has "out-called" the ecclesia, which is here referred to as Christ's *Body*. The Body of Christ is the <u>complement</u> of the One completing the all in all (1:23).

Remember that a "complement" is something that completes the whole. Christ is the One commissioned by God to bring all into subjection to Him so that He will ultimately become all in all, and the Body of Christ is the complement to Christ in this process.

How does the Body of Christ serve as Christ's complement?

I think the best description is found in 2 Corinthians 5:18-21. *Yet all is of God, Who conciliates us to Himself through Christ, and is giving us the dispensation of the conciliation, how that God was in Christ, conciliating the world to Himself, not reckoning their offenses to them, and placing in us the word of the conciliation. For Christ, then, are we ambassadors, as of God entreating through us. We are beseeching for Christ's sake, 'Be conciliated to God!'*

We are charged, then, with announcing the fact that God has, through Christ, become conciliated to man. Despite man's wickedness and sin, because of Christ God is now conciliated to man and is not reckoning man's offenses to him.

But all are not yet conciliated to God. Much of mankind is alienated from God. There is not yet <u>reconciliation</u>, but only a one-sided conciliation on God's part. We are charged, as ambassadors, to proclaim as if God were proclaiming through us, *Be conciliated to God!* This is the part we play as Christ's complement.

And when, in fact, all have become conciliated to God ... some by faith in this current era, and others by sight in an era to come ... there will be a total and complete reconciliation. All will be subjected to God through the work of Christ (the One completing the all in all) and His complement (the Body of Christ), and then we will see the triumphant conclusion to the eons when God becomes all in all (1 Corinthians 15:28).

Milestones in Paul's Ministry *(The Pause)*

> Trail Marker #54
> ## The Body in the Celestials (2:4)

Yet God, being rich in mercy, because of His vast love with which He loves us (we also being dead to the offenses and the lusts), vivifies us together in Christ (in grace are you saved!) and rouses us together and seats us together among the celestials, in Christ Jesus, that, in the oncoming eons, He should be displaying the transcendent riches of His grace in His kindness to us in Christ Jesus.

So despite the fact that we were just as the rest of humanity, walking in sin and the lusts of the flesh, children of indignation even in our very nature, God saves us and vivifies us (makes us alive) and seats us in the celestials. We are no better than the rest of humanity, yet God displays His grace and mercy in this way. Why would God do this?

Remember that God desired to have a complement to Christ, the One completing the all in all. We also see another part of the reason why God chose a subset of humanity to be His ecclesia. *That, in the oncoming eons, He will display the riches of His grace and kindness* (2:7). While we serve as ambassadors and Christ's complement in this present eon, in the coming eon when God seats us in the celestials (the heavens), all of creation will come to see God's grace and mercy through this display.

Our expectation in the eon to come is not here upon this earth. We do not await Christ to return to reign. We await His call to meet Him in the air (1 Thessalonians 4:13-18) and to serve our place in the celestials, where we will be a display of God's grace and mercy.

As for now, Christ is already seated in the celestials, having been roused from among the dead. We in the Body of Christ have *figuratively* been roused and vivified and are seated in the celestials, but we have not yet fully realized this in a literal way. One day, though, we too will be roused from among the dead (just as Christ, the Firstfruit) and seated in the celestials.

Milestones in Paul's Ministry *(The Pause)*

> Trail Marker #55
>
> ## A new humanity (2:11)

Remember that once you, the nations in flesh; termed Uncircumcision by those termed Circumcision; you were in that era, apart from Christ, being alienated from the citizenship of Israel, and guests of the promise covenants, having no expectation ...

In the past the nations had no expectation as did Israel, and at best were only guests of the promise covenants. But Paul now announces a new humanity.

Yet now, in Christ Jesus, you; once far off; are become near by the blood of Christ. For He is our Peace, Who makes both one, and razes the central wall of the barrier; nullifying the law of precepts in decrees, that He should be creating the two, in Himself, into one new humanity; reconciling both in one body.

The barrier between Israel and the nations has been razed, and the law of precepts in decrees (Israel's law) has been nullified. What had been two (Israel and the nations; the Circumcision and the Uncircumcision) has now been created into one new humanity; one body.

Consequently, then, no longer are you guests and sojourners, but are fellow-citizens of the saints and belong to God's family.

This is a new proclamation. Always in the past God has worked through Israel as His chosen people. Those of the nations could only enjoy the covenants by sojourning with Israel and observing the law that was given to Israel.

In His earthly ministry Jesus came to the sheep of Israel. The ministry of the Twelve was to the sheep of Israel. Even the apostle Paul would always go first to Israel, and only after being rejected would he approach the Gentiles.

Not so any longer. God now has a new creation; the Body of Christ, comprised of Jew and Gentile with no barrier, preference or distinction.

This is something new, not proclaimed in the past. We see this good news only in Paul's writings. It had not been revealed to others before Paul; not even by Christ Himself during His earthly ministry.

This is why Paul found it necessary to note that his evangel was not something he learned from man; it was revealed to him by Christ (Galatians 1:12). This is why Paul refers to this as a secret. (3:1-5) And this is why Paul was so strongly opposed by Jews who believed but were zealous for the law (Acts 21:20).

Can we therefore understand why it is so crucial to rightly divide the Scriptures? (2 Timothy 2:15)

If we choose from the writings of the Twelve which were directed to Israel without distinguishing them from the writings of Paul which were directed to the Body of Christ, we would be mixing together two different things, and we would fail to understand this <u>secret</u> that Paul shares with us.

God is moving beyond what He had established through Israel; which was the basis of the entire Old Testament, the four Gospels, most of the book of Acts, and the letters from the Circumcision apostles; and He has now proclaimed something new and far superior and advanced through Paul.

> Trail Marker #56
> ## Revealing the secret (3:3)

For by revelation the secret is made known to me (according as I write before, in brief, by which you who are reading are able to apprehend my understanding in the secret of the Christ, which, in other generations, is not made known to the sons of humanity as it was now revealed to His holy apostles and prophets). In spirit the nations are to be joint enjoyers of an allotment, and a joint body, and joint partakers of the promise in Christ Jesus, through the evangel of which I became the dispenser.

Again we see that Paul's gospel is not the same as the gospel that had been shared by the apostles before him. The gospel he shares was <u>revealed</u> to him; it was <u>a secret not made known to others before him</u>. It was granted to Paul;

To bring the evangel of the untraceable riches of Christ to the nations, and to enlighten all as to what is the administration of the secret, which has been concealed from the eons in God, Who creates all, that now may be made known to the sovereignties and the authorities among the celestials, through the ecclesia, the multifarious wisdom of God, in accord with the purpose of the eons.

That which Paul now reveals concerning the Body of Christ is <u>untraceable</u>. It is not something that man could have discerned on his own from God's previous revelation, since it was a secret that had been concealed in the past and is only now revealed through Paul.

Even those in the celestial (heavenly) realm did not see this coming. God's wisdom was not fully revealed until now.

If what Paul writes here is true; if this is a secret that God had concealed in times past and that is now being revealed; how can we possibly think Paul is sharing the same gospel (good news) that others before him had shared (i.e. the Twelve)?

It may seem as though God's plan was failing. God chose Israel and provided the law to set His chosen people apart. But Israel could not keep the law.

How could God save mankind from a final death when even the means provided to rescue man (the law, and Israel) had failed.

But now we see an even greater wisdom that had not previously been made known; a multifarious wisdom in accord with the purpose of the eons. This, then, is the purpose of the eons; the purpose of the history of God's dealings with mankind; to bring us to this point where now we are ready to see the unveiling of this secret that is far superior to anything God has revealed before.

It is not just Israel that God has chosen, with dictates of law to be observed (which Israel found impossible to observe). The Body of Christ has now been revealed; those of all nations with no preference or distinction, for the purpose of serving as Christ's complement to bring about the total subjection of all mankind to God, that God may become All in all.

Those of us who are within the Body of Christ find ourselves here only because of God's grace. We have done nothing to deserve this. We are no better than the balance of mankind. We find ourselves in this position only to display God's grace to all of creation, both in the heavens and upon the earth, and to serve as Christ's ambassadors in proclaiming the evangel that is intended for this era, and in doing so we are acting as Christ's complement in bringing about God becoming all in all.

Milestones in Paul's Ministry *(The Pause)*

> Trail Marker #57
> ## For the eon of the eons (3:21)

To Him be glory in the ecclesia and in Christ Jesus for all the generations *of the eon of the eons.*

Consider this phrase. Eon (singular) and eons (plural) are often translated "endless" or "eternal." But if eon is intended to express endlessness, why is the plural form needed? And what would a phrase like eon of the eons mean? Clearly eon is a period of time that has a beginning and an end, and since the plural is used we know there are multiple periods of time being referred to. In this present case reference is made to a single eon (the present eon in which we live) as compared with all of the eons.

When Bible translations fail to distinguish things like this, and when these distinct periods of time are simply mixed together into "eternity," how can we ever hope to fully understand all that God has revealed to us?

We must go beyond the modern English versions and use study tools that are available to seek out truth. Young's Analytical Concordance, for example, will help us to search individual words as they appear in the Greek, not just as the words have been translated into English. The Concordant Literal New Testament with the Keyword Concordance will also let us go beyond the English translation and consider the precise distinctions made in the original Greek.

If we are to understand truth and share the correct message with the world today as Christ's ambassadors, we cannot place our faith in Bible translators who clearly disagree with each other in many passages.

> ## Trail Marker #58
> ## The systematizing of the deception (4:14)

That we may by no means still be minors, surging hither and thither and being carried about by every wind of teaching, by human caprice, by craftiness with a view to <u>the systematizing of the deception</u>.

Paul refers here to those using human caprice and craftiness with the intent of deceiving in a systemic manner. What could this possibly refer to other than those within organized religion?

Consider that by the end of Paul's lifetime he had been abandoned by nearly everyone (2 Timothy 1:15; 4:16; Acts 21:20). There were those who had been proclaiming a different evangel; a distortion of the evangel (Galatians 1:7). There were those who followed Paul everywhere to distort his evangel of grace and freedom from the law, attempting to integrate the law into the evangel.

The majority within "organized religion" were working against Paul, as they did not understand the evangel that God had revealed to him, which was different from the evangel that had been previously revealed and proclaimed by others.

Remember that Jesus, too, was opposed by "organized religion" during His earthly ministry. And the prophets of the Old Testament were often opposed by "organized religion" in their day.

We live in a day of apostasy, as both Peter and Paul warned of in their later letters; where the majority within "organized religion" do not understand that which God has revealed. They attempt to systematize (or "religion-ize") deception through organized structure and teachings. This is, in my opinion, the systematizing of the deception that Paul refers to in 4:14; and it is still alive today.

If the Deceiver can "systematize deception" (4:14) – deceiving in an organized fashion that appears to be legitimate and true – can he not prevent the secret of the evangel from being recognized? If the Deceiver can allow the evangel of grace to be distorted by adding elements of the law, even as was done among the Galatians in Paul's day, can he not hide the secret of the evangel that Paul is sharing in Ephesians? If the Deceiver can cause Peter's message to the Circumcision believers to be mixed with the different message that Paul proclaimed to the Body of Christ, can he not prevent the secret of the evangel from being proclaimed?

I personally believe that all of these things are accomplished by the Deceiver, in a systematized fashion, through the organized church today. Orthodox teachings that are passed from one generation to the next without challenge, contaminated Bible translations, churches, pastors, Bible teachers, mainstream Christian authors, seminaries and Bible colleges that simply pass "truth" along to every new generation of believers; all of these things have worked together to systematize deception; to prevent the Body of Christ from recognizing the secret of the evangel and from serving its role as the complement of Christ.

I am convinced that to recognize the secret of the evangel and to fulfill our role as Christ's complement, we must escape the bonds of organized religion and its experts and authorities, turning to the Word of God in its purest form.

> ### Trail Marker #59
> ### Spiritual forces (6:11)

Put on the panoply of God, to enable you to stand up to the stratagems of the Adversary, for it is not ours to wrestle with blood and flesh, but with the sovereignties, with the authorities, with the world-mights of this darkness, with the spiritual forces of wickedness among the celestials. Therefore take up the panoply of God that you may be enabled to withstand in the wicked day.

There is more to this universe than what is visible to our eyes of flesh. In the celestial realm there is a created order, and some of it is wicked. The struggles we face are not always driven by the obvious; the things that we can see.

Therefore we must be on guard and equip ourselves with spiritual mechanisms that God has provided if we are to stand in the midst of these struggles.

Truth, righteousness, the evangel of peace, faith, salvation, and the declaration (or word) of God.

By way of example, when the wicked one attacks with his fiery arrows that challenge what we know to be truth as revealed by God, faith is our shield (6:16-17). If we allow our faith to go un-nurtured we will succumb to the challenges we are faced with (that are coming from spiritual forces). We will lose our faith and will be unable to stand and perform our role as Christ's complement.

It is because of our role as Christ's complement that we receive challenges from the celestial realm; for the spiritual forces of wickedness among the celestials (6:12) are working against the plans of God. Since we play a part in those plans, we can expect challenges from the celestial realm that seek to prevent us from serving our role.

Milestones in Paul's Ministry *(The Pause)*

> **Trail Marker #60**
> ## Paul's Ephesian ministry in Acts

Consider the difference between Paul's Ephesian ministry (as recorded in Acts) and his letter to the Ephesians which came much later.

In Paul's early ministry he describes his role as "competent dispensers of a new covenant" (2 Corinthians 3:6) and a "priest" (Romans 15:16), both related to Israel and not his later ministry to the Body of Christ. During that time Paul spoke to the sheep of Israel scattered among the nations, baptizing (Acts 19:5-6) and performing miracles (Acts 19:11). During that time he spoke only things that the prophets and Moses had previously shared (Acts 26:22).

But after the setting aside of Israel (Acts 28:28; Romans 11:25) and while imprisoned in Rome, Paul shared new truth that had been revealed to him by Christ Jesus; and we find this new truth in his letter to the Ephesians. In this letter he spoke of new things such as being blessed among the celestials (1:3; 1:20), secrets (1:9; 3:3; 3:4; 3:9), the Body (1:23; 2:16; 3:6), a new humanity (2:15), and no barrier between those of Israel and those of the nations (2:14).

With these stark contrasts we see the progressive revelation from God unfold. And we see the need to rightly divide the Word of God (2 Timothy 2:15) lest we attempt to apply truth from a previous era to a later era; thereby misunderstanding how God is working!

Philippians

> Trail Marker #61
> ## Test the things of consequence (1:10)

Be testing what things are of consequence, that you may be sincere and no stumbling block.

This is as if to say, don't argue over lesser things, and in so doing become contentious and a stumbling block to those observing this behavior, but focus on the important things of consequence.

Milestones in Paul's Ministry *(The Pause)*

> **Trail Marker #62**
>
> ## Confidence in the flesh? (3:4)

If any presume to have confidence in flesh, I rather. I was circumcised, an Israelite of the tribe of Benjamin, a Hebrew of Hebrews, a Pharisee, zealous, and a keeper of the law. But all of this I forfeit and consider refuse because of Christ.

Not having my righteousness out of law; but that which is through the faith of Christ, the righteousness which is from God, FOR faith.

Our confidence is not to be on our talents, abilities, education, degrees, or anything of a fleshly accomplishment. All such is refuse because of Christ. The righteousness we have is all of Christ.

Colossians

> ### Trail Marker #63
> ### Walk worthily (1:10)

Paul's desire is that the believers fully realize God's will (1:9), *in all wisdom and spiritual understanding ...* and that they <u>walk worthily</u> *of the Lord for all pleasing, bearing fruit in every good work, and growing in the realization of God; for all endurance and patience with joy.*

It is possible, then, to have a realization of God and His grace; but not a FULL realization. Paul's prayer is for the believers to grow into a FULL realization, and to walk worthily.

Milestones in Paul's Ministry *(The Pause)*

> ### Trail Marker #64
> ## All created – All reconciled (1:16)

In Him is all created; that in the heavens and earth; visible and invisible; whether thrones, lordships, sovereignties or authorities. All is created through Him and for Him, and He is before all, and all has its cohesion in Him.

As it pertains to believers ...

Christ is the Head of the body, the ecclesia. Sovereign, Firstborn from among the dead, that in all He may be becoming first. For in Him the entire complement delights to dwell.

As it pertains to all creation ...

Through Him to reconcile all to Him; whether those on the earth or those in the heavens; making peace through the blood of His cross.

In Him ALL is created. Through Him ALL is reconciled!

Remember the ALL in this context, from 1:14, refers to all of creation. Believers (the Body, or ecclesia) are noted in a special way, but *all* refers to all of creation.

The reconciliation in 1:20 is a parallel to the creation in 1:14. All are created; and through Christ all are to be reconciled. This is the CLIMAX of God's reconciliation with His entire creation!

So we see that all creation will ultimately be reconciled. At present the ecclesia (Body of Christ) is reconciled. Remember the differentiation as seen in 2 Corinthians 5:18-21 between conciliation (one-sided) and reconciliation (two-sided). The 2 Corinthians passage tells us that in Christ, God was conciliating the world to Himself. But the world is not yet conciliated to God. The world is estranged from God. Our proclamation, as Christ's ambassadors, is: "Be conciliated to God!" Those heeding that call, and who become conciliated to God, would then be reconciled.

And, as we see in Colossians 1:20, through Christ will ALL be reconciled.

Milestones in Paul's Ministry *(The Pause)*

> Trail Marker #65
> ## To <u>complete</u> the word of God ^(1:25)

I became a dispenser, in accord with the administration of God, which is granted to me for you, <u>to complete the word of God</u>; the secret which has been concealed from the eons and from the generations, yet now was made manifest to His saints, to whom God wills to make known that are the glorious riches of this secret among the nations ...

This is a major point, not to be overlooked!

In the past God spoke through certain individuals he had chosen; Moses, Abraham, Isaac, Jacob. He spoke through the prophets of the Old Testament. He spoke most directly through His Son, Jesus Christ.

And after the crucifixion and resurrection God spoke through prophets in the early ecclesia.

Now comes Paul, who informs us that he has come to COMPLETE the word of God. After this point there would no longer be the need for prophecy or prophets, for the word of God would now be complete. The Scriptures preserved by the apostles (including Paul) say it all! There would be nothing to add to what had already been revealed.

Did Paul not tell us that prophesies, at some point, would be discarded and languages (tongues) would cease? (1 Corinthians 13:8)

Milestones in Paul's Ministry *(The Pause)*

> Trail Marker #66
>
> ## Paul's secret (1:26)

Note that as Paul completes the word of God, he reveals a SECRET. This is proof that Paul's message was different, and not the same as that of the Twelve; else it would not be a secret that had been concealed in the past.

Christ among you, the expectation of glory, Whom we are announcing, admonishing every man and teaching every man in all wisdom that we should be presenting every man mature in Christ Jesus.

There are other mentions in Paul's writings of a secret, and to gain a complete understanding of the secret(s) revealed by Paul we should study all passages where this is noted. As for what we are told concerning the secret in this current passage … there is a need for growth and maturity in the Body of Christ (unlike the immaturity and fleshliness that Paul confronted in 1 Corinthians).

Turning once again to 1 Corinthians 13:8, where Paul tells us of a time when prophecies will be discarded and languages will cease, we note that this would happen when maturity comes (1 Corinthians 13:10). And now in Colossians, as Paul announces his charge to complete the word of God, we see his additional charge to present every man mature in Christ Jesus.

As maturity comes, and as the word of God is completed, there is no longer a need for the inferior devices (prophecy, languages) to guide believers.

Milestones in Paul's Ministry *(The Pause)*

> Trail Marker #67
> ## Beware of philosophy & tradition (2:8)

Beware that no one shall be despoiling you through philosophy and empty seduction, in accord with human tradition, in accord with the elements of the world, and not in accord with Christ. And you are complete in Him.

Believers are complete in Christ. Nothing is to be added to God's grace. No law, rules or regulations are needed. Paul introduces maturity and completion; the believer is complete in Christ.

"Religion" in all ages has incorporated much philosophy and human tradition. Beware of religion. Cling simply to the truth as revealed by God in His completed Word.

Let no one, then, be judging you in food or in drink or in the particulars of a festival, or of a new moon, or of sabbaths, which are a shadow of those things which are impending – yet the body is the Christ's. (2:16)

In short; all of these outward and visible "do's and don'ts" served their purpose but are not to be enforced upon the Body of Christ.

If, then, you died together with Christ from the elements of the world, why, as living in the world, are you subject to decrees: "You should not be touching, nor yet tasting, nor yet coming into contact," ... in accord with the directions and teachings of men?

Religious circles today are filled with requirements and rituals. Churchgoers are convinced that they must celebrate "the sabbath" by attending worship services, abstaining from work, etc. Many are convinced they must be water baptized. Is it not clear from what Paul is saying here that these things do not matter? Christ has surpassed these things, yet religious leaders continue to impose elements of the law upon believers.

Observe once again verse 8; BEWARE of human tradition!

> ## Trail Marker #68
> ## Behavior (3:1)

To start with ... *seek that which is above.*

If, then, you were roused together with Christ, be seeking that which is above, where Christ is, sitting at the right hand of God. Be disposed to that which is above, not to that on the earth, for you died.

Since we figuratively died with Christ and were roused with Him, there is no longer a need or requirement for us to be disposed to earthly things; like the law, feasts and festivals, sabbaths, dietary restrictions. And we are also to set aside other earth-bound characteristics ...

Deaden, then, your members that are on the earth: prostitution, uncleanness, passion, evil desire and greed, which is idolatry, because of which the indignation of God is coming on the sons of stubbornness – among whom you also once walked when you lived in these things.

Those within the world will one day face the indignation of God (Romans 2:9) on the day of indignation (Romans 2:5) because of these behaviors. Paul is not saying that believers will also face God's indignation if they persist in these behaviors. Salvation is not based upon works, but God's grace. God has called the Body of Christ for special work that will ultimately contribute toward reconciling the entire world to God; and we are spared from this coming indignation (Romans 5:9).

What Paul is saying in this passage is: "Since these behaviors will result in God's indignation upon those of the world, and since we have been spared from the day of indignation by God's grace, let us not walk in these same behaviors."

Some specific behaviors to "put away" ... (3:8)

Be putting away anger, fury, malice, calumny, obscenity, and lying.

Why is this important if we have been saved by grace, and not works?

Milestones in Paul's Ministry *(The Pause)*

To accord with the Image of the One Who creates it, wherein there is no Greek and Jew, Circumcision and Uncircumcision, barbarian, Scythian, slave, freeman, but all and in all is Christ.

Some specific behaviors to "put on" ...

Put on, as God's chosen ones; pitiful compassions, kindness, humility, meekness, and patience (bearing with one another and dealing graciously among yourselves as the Lord deals graciously with you).

And above all these put on love, which is the tie of maturity.

Become thankful. Let the word of Christ be making its home in you richly, in all wisdom, teaching and admonishing yourselves.

Everything you do, in word or act, do all in the name of the Lord Jesus Christ, giving thanks to God.

Notice that it is the word of Christ that teaches and admonishes us, not a priest, pastor or minister. In times past, before maturity, these fleshly designates were needed to teach and admonish. But Paul's words in Colossians are of a higher nature, and it is the word of Christ that now teaches and admonishes without the need for a mediator.

Milestones in Paul's Ministry *(The Pause)*

> Trail Marker #69
> # No Greek or Jew ... (3:11)

There is no Greek and Jew, Circumcision and Uncircumcision, barbarian, Scythian, slave, freeman, but all and in all is Christ.

This is a key difference in Paul's writings!

ALWAYS before this time Israel had been primary. The Gentile could only be blessed through Israel. During Jesus' earthly ministry He came only to the sheep of Israel. Even in Paul's early ministry he would go first to the synagogues, and only to the Gentile when Israel rejected his message.

But now, clearly, there is a difference. Paul, and only Paul, revealed the Body of Christ; God's chosen ones (3:12) within which there is no longer a superiority granted to Israel. This is clearly different from the teachings of the entire Old Testament, the four Gospel accounts, and the ministry and epistles of the Twelve.

Paul is the apostle to the Gentiles, and his message is clearly different from all that preceded him.

1 Thessalonians

> ## Trail Marker #70
> ## Rescued out of coming indignation (1:10)

... waiting for His Son out of the heavens; our Rescuer out of the coming indignation.

So ... what were the Thessalonians awaiting and expecting? They were waiting for the Son out of the heavens; their Rescuer out of the coming indignation.

Clearly there is a coming indignation, but the ecclesia is saved from that indignation.

Indignation was coming upon the world (Romans 2:9) on the day of indignation that is set by God (Romans 2:5). But the believer is saved from this coming indignation (Romans 5:9) by our Rescuer out of the coming indignation (1 Thessalonians 1:10).

We within the Body of Christ are saved from the coming indignation not because we are better than others of humanity; but because God has elected to choose a subset of humanity; giving them the ability to believe and perceive that which He has revealed; and enabling them to serve as a complement of Christ in this age and in the ages to come; toward the end that God's will for mankind be accomplished; that all mankind be saved and come to a realization of the truth (1 Timothy 2:4).

Milestones in Paul's Ministry *(The Pause)*

> Trail Marker #71
>
> **Walk worthily** (2:12)

Be walking worthily of God, Who calls you into His own kingdom and glory.

Far from threatening the believers if they failed to have faith, Paul simply *encourages* them to be walking worthily of God.

But we see that Paul is not concerned only with doctrine at the expense of behavior.

And we see that despite the fact that we are not under the law and our standing is entirely due to God's grace ... proper behavior is still important to Paul. There is right behavior and there is wrong behavior; and Paul never shies away from encouraging the believers to walk worthily.

> **Trail Marker #72**
> ## Paul's word is the word of God (2:13)

In accepting the word heard from us, from God you receive not the word of men but the word of God, as it truly is; operating in you who are believing.

So the writings of Paul that we find in the Scriptures are to be treated no less than any of the other writings found there. His writings are the word of God.

We also see here a distinction between the believer and unbeliever. While the word of God may be *heard* by those who are not believing, it is *operating* in the believer. This must be so, in order to equip the believer for the task to which he is called by God.

Trail Marker #73
The snatching away (4:13-18)

Paul wanted the believers to understand their expectation ...

We do not want you to be ignorant, brethren, concerning those who are reposing, lest you may sorrow according as the rest, also, who have no expectation.

It is not that the believer does not sorrow. He sorrows in a different way than those outside the ecclesia because he possesses an expectation that those outside do not recognize. The believer knows with <u>certainty</u> what will take place in the ages to come. This, then, is one of the distinctives in believing.

For, if we are believing that Jesus died and rose, thus also, those who are put to repose, will God, through Jesus, lead forth together with Him. For this we are saying to you by the word of the Lord, that we, the living, who are surviving to the presence of the Lord, should by no means outstrip those who are put to repose, for the Lord Himself will be descending from heaven with a shout of command, with the voice of the Chief Messenger, and with the trumpet of God, and the dead in Christ shall be rising first.

The expectation of the Body of Christ is this "snatching away" to meet the Lord in the air. There will come a day when the trumpet sounds and the believers who had previously died will be resurrected.

Thereupon we, the living who are surviving, shall at the same time be SNATCHED AWAY together with them in clouds, to meet the Lord in the air. And thus shall we always be together with the Lord.

Commonly known as "the rapture," here is the moment when Christ calls the Body of Christ to be with Him. Those still living at this time do not die but are snatched away into the clouds to be with the Lord; reunited with those who had previously died who are resurrected and also snatched away.

So that, console one another with these words.

Knowing this day is coming is our expectation and it enables us to mourn our losses differently than those outside the ecclesia that do not share this expectation.

This is not to say that those outside the ecclesia will not also be resurrected. This will occur at a subsequent time. But because the Body of Christ has been called, in part, to serve God's purposes in the heavenly realm in the ages to come, we are called first on this day described to the Thessalonians.

> Trail Marker #74
>
> ## The Day of the Lord (5:2)

The Day of the Lord is as a thief in the night. They may say that all is peaceful and secure, yet extermination will come. But you are not in darkness about these events so as to be overtaken as a thief. Consequently; be watching and sober; and not drowsing.

So while others may be ignorant about what will take place when the Day of the Lord comes, the believer is not.

We, being of the day, may be sober, putting on the cuirass of faith and love, and the helmet, the expectation of salvation, for God did not appoint us to indignation but to the procuring of salvation through our Lord Jesus Christ, Who died for our sakes, that, whether we may be watching or drowsing, we should be living at the same time together with Him.

The Day of the Lord is different from the day of "the snatching away."

It is a time when there will be extermination (death) and indignation. But the believer can have faith and love because God did not appoint us to indignation. First will come the snatching away of the ecclesia, whereupon we will be with the Lord; and then will come the Day of The Lord upon the earth.

And with this knowledge; this expectation of what lies ahead; whether we may be watching or drowsing, we should be living at the same time together with Him.

Our salvation and rescue from indignation is not dependent on our being watchful. We are called to be watchful and sober (not drowsing and drunk), but even if we fail to be watchful we are living with Him; both figuratively in the present age, and literally once we are snatched away to be with Him.

> **Trail Marker #75**
> **Behavior (again)** (5:13)

- ✓ *Be at peace among yourselves.*
- ✓ *Admonish the disorderly.*
- ✓ *Comfort the faint-hearted.*
- ✓ *Uphold the infirm.*
- ✓ *Be patient toward all.*
- ✓ *See that no one may be rendering evil for evil.*
- ✓ *Always pursue that which is good for one another as well as for all.*
- ✓ *Be rejoicing always.*
- ✓ *Be praying unintermittingly.*
- ✓ *In everything be giving thanks.*
- ✓ *Quench not the spirit.*
- ✓ *Scorn not prophecies.*
- ✓ *Be testing all, retaining the ideal.*
- ✓ *Abstain from everything wicked to the perception.*

Relative to Paul's statement concerning prophecies, this is an indication that the letter to the Thessalonians was an earlier letter than Colossians, where Paul indicates that he was charged with completing the word of God. Once Paul completed that commission, could it be that prophecy was no longer required, since the word from God had been completed?

2 Thessalonians

> ## Trail Marker #76
> ## Day of the Lord not yet here (2:2)

Don't be shaken in your mind or alarmed through spirit or word or an epistle; that the Day of the Lord is present. No one should be deluding you.

Some in their midst were declaring that the Day of the Lord was already present, but Paul warns them not to be deluded.

The Day of the Lord is that time, following the removal of the Body of Christ unto the heavens (1 Thessalonians 4:13ff), when the events immediately preceding and culminating with the return of Christ to the earth will take place.

Could this same warning be valid today? Some today claim that the Day of the Lord has already come, just as some were saying in Paul's day. Did the Day of the Lord commence since the time of Paul's writing to the Thessalonians? I think not, based on what Paul says next ...

The apostasy will come first, and the man of lawlessness will be revealed; the son of destruction who is opposing and lifting himself up over everyone called a god, so that he is seated in the temple of God demonstrating that he is God.

Certain things must occur prior to the Day of the Lord. The apostasy must come first, and the man of lawlessness must be unveiled; seated in the temple of God, demonstrating that he is God.

He will be unveiled in his own era. The secret of lawlessness is already operating, but only when the present <u>detainer</u> may be coming out of the midst, then the lawless one will be unveiled – the one whom the Lord Jesus will discard by the advent of His presence.

The lawless one's presence is in accord with the operation of Satan, with all power and signs and false miracles, and with every seduction of injustice among those who are perishing, because they do not receive the love of the truth for their salvation. So God will send them a deception, for them to believe the falsehood, that all may be judged who do not believe the truth but delight in injustice.

Note there is a "detainer." Something is detaining the man of lawlessness.

While the secret of lawlessness is already operating, <u>the man of lawlessness has not yet been unveiled</u>. He will be unveiled in his own era, but only when the present detainer may be coming to be out of the midst. And then the man of lawlessness will be unveiled and will exhibit power and signs and false miracles. We read of this all taking place in the book of Revelation, when the Day of the Lord comes.

From this description and coupled with Paul's mention of the Body of Christ's removal from the earth in 1 Thessalonians 4:13ff, it seems that the detainer that Paul mentions here is the Body of Christ, or more probably the holy spirit that is operating within the Body of Christ. Once this is removed from the earth, the man of lawlessness will be unveiled, and the Day of the Lord will commence.

Milestones in Paul's Ministry *(The Pause)*

> Trail Marker #77
> ## Work (3:8)

We did not eat bread gratuitously from anyone, but with toil and labor, we are working night and day, so as not to be burdensome to any of you.

Not that we have not the right, but that we might be giving you ourselves as a model to be imitating. Even when we were with you we charged: <u>If anyone is not willing to work, neither let him eat</u>.

Paul had the right to ask for their support, but he voluntarily forfeited that right and instead became a model to be imitated.

Milestones in Paul's Ministry *(The Pause)*

> Trail Marker #78
>
> ## The disorderly (3:11)

We are hearing that some among you are walking disorderly, working at nothing, but meddling. We are charging and entreating you to work with quietness, eating your own bread.

Don't be despondent in ideal doing. If anyone is not obeying our word through this epistle, <u>don't commingle with him</u>. Don't deem him as an enemy but admonish him as a brother.

While the disorderly are to be admonished, they are to be admonished as a brother; not deemed as an enemy. The one who is not heeding Paul's words has not lost his salvation and is not excommunicated as a "member of the church;" but he is to be cast out of fellowship of the brethren.

++

1 Timothy

Note that this is a personal letter to one man; Timothy. Thus it differs from Paul's letters to this point that were directed to the ecclesia in various places. We must take care to distinguish between general truths for the ecclesia, and those things intended for one man (Timothy) in his unique position.

Trail Marker #79
Some want to teach the law ^(1:5)

The consummation of our charge is love out of a clean heart, a good conscience, and unfeigned faith, from which some are swerving and exhibit vain prating, <u>wanting to be teachers of the law</u>.

The law is ideal if it is used lawfully. The law is not laid down for the just, but for the lawless, the insubordinate, the irreverent, sinners, the malign and profane, thrashers of mothers and fathers, homicides, paramours, sodomites, kidnapers, liars, perjurers, and all others that oppose sound teaching in accord with the evangel of the glory of the happy God, with which I am entrusted.

The law is not laid down for the just. We recall that the believer is justified (Romans 3:28, Romans 5:1, Galatians 2:16, Galatians 3:23-25), and is dead to the law and to sin (Romans 7:1-6, Galatians 2:19), so the use of the law among believers is not proper.

While some of the behaviors noted by Paul unfortunately exist among believers, his point is that the purpose of the law was to address these issues among the unrighteous. Later came the implementation of God's grace in a more powerful way; justifying the believer, freeing him from the law, and reckoning him as dead to sin and alive in Christ.

In short, there is no place for the law in the midst of this grace. Paul fought the commingling of law and grace in Galatians, and he continues to fight it here.

> Trail Marker #80
> ## Paul is a "pattern" (1:12-16)

I am grateful to Christ Jesus our Lord who invigorates me and deems me faithful, assigning me a service. I was formerly a calumniator, a persecutor, and an outrager. But I was shown mercy, seeing that I do it in ignorance and unbelief. But the Lord's grace <u>overwhelms</u> with faith and love.

Christ Jesus came into the world to save sinners, foremost of whom am I. But therefore I was shown mercy, that in me, the foremost, Jesus Christ should be displaying all His patience, for a <u>pattern</u> of those who are about to be believing on Him for life eonian.

Did you catch this?

Under the "old rules" Paul's opposition and persecution of Christ would have warranted rejection and wrath. This is often preached today; rejection and wrath upon those that fail to believe.

Yet Paul who deserved rejection and wrath was instead shown mercy, and his case became a PATTERN for others who would be led to believe.

Will any escape this mercy? Remember Paul's words; the grace of our Lord *overwhelms*.

Milestones in Paul's Ministry *(The Pause)*

> Trail Marker #81
>
> # King of the eons (1:17)

Now to the <u>King of the eons</u>, the incorruptible, invisible, only, and wise God, be honor and glory <u>for the eons of the eons</u>!

In verses 16-17 the Greek AION is used in a variety of interesting forms. Those believing will find life eonian. To translate this eternal life would be an incorrect manipulation of the Greek. The point here is that believers will experience life in the eons to come.

This does not mean that life will cease once the eons have concluded. The believer will put on immortality (1 Corinthians 15:54) and will therefore continue to live at the conclusion of the eons. But the point of this present passage is that the believer will have life in the eons to come.

Let us not alter the Greek by injecting our theological understandings. Let us instead seek to render the Greek accurately, lest we fail to correctly handle the Scriptures and hinder our ability to understand God's revelation to us.

In verse 17 Paul uses the phrase *King of the eons*. Some say this proves that eons (plural) must mean forever, since Christ is immortal. Again; let us not inject our theological understandings into the translation effort.

I have five children; Cris, Dusty, Chad, Kari and Scott. When I find myself among Chad's friends I may say, "I am the father of Chad." Does this mean I am not also the father of my other four children? No; it is simply that in that context of Chad's friends I seek to identify myself as his father. So also in the context of the eons; these finite periods of time in which man's history is recorded in the Scriptures; Christ is the King of the eons.

Lastly, in verse 17 we see the phrase *for the eons of the eons*. If eon (singular) or eons (plural) means eternity, then what purpose would there be in saying eons of the eons? If we fail to notice the distinctions in the various forms of aion as used in the Greek, and if we simply inject our theological understandings regardless of the form; saying eternal when that seems to fit and age when eternal clearly does not fit the context; then we will fail to grasp the rich meaning of God's revelation to us.

A close study of the Scriptures seems to tell us of five distinct eons or ages in the history of mankind. Eon (singular) is speaking of one of these periods of time. Eons (plural) speaks of more than one of these periods of time. Eons of the eons is like saying "two or more ages in particular, in the context of all five ages" (if five is the correct number; that is simply my observation).

The last two eons are those following the return of Christ to the earth. Paul is emphasizing these two glorious eons in his benediction; Now to the King of the eons, the incorruptible, invisible, only, and wise God, be honor and glory for the eons of the eons! Amen!

> ## Trail Marker #82
> ## God's will – The salvation of all (2:4-7)

God, <u>Who wills that all mankind be saved</u> and come into a realization of the truth.

For there is one God, and one Mediator of God and mankind, a Man, Christ Jesus, Who is giving Himself <u>a correspondent Ransom for all</u> (the <u>testimony in its own eras</u>), for which I was appointed a herald and an apostle; a teacher of the nations.

Consider closely these words, for they are clearly contrary to the common orthodox belief in eternal torment.

It is God's will that ALL MANKIND be saved. Remember also that God is operating all things in accord with His will (Ephesians 1:11). That being the case, what can prevent the salvation of all from happening?

Some say it is man's stubborn, free will that stands in the way; but are we saying that the Creator is unable to lead every last one of mankind into a realization of the truth, if that is His will?

Remember that Paul refers to the Lord's grace as <u>overwhelming</u>, and Paul himself was most certainly led in a very overwhelming way to the truth on the road to Damascus.

Consider also that Christ is a "<u>correspondent ransom</u>."

Some say that if all are saved then Christ's death upon the Cross becomes unnecessary. Far from that! It is not only necessary, but far more effectual than orthodoxy would claim.

For Christ gave Himself as a correspondent Ransom for all (not just for some). Just as death came to all mankind through Adam, so life comes to all mankind through Christ, the correspondent, one-for-one Ransom for all.

Correspondent ransom differs from the simple notion of ransom. The thought expressed in the Greek is the idea of equivalence. It is a one-for-one (i.e. "correspondent") ransom of all mankind.

Consider also ... What is meant by the <u>testimony in its own eras</u>? (1:6)

I believe this means that the *realization* of the truth by all mankind is a progressive thing. Some of us have been gifted with faith in this present age, but others do not yet see. But they will see in a future era.

As Christ's Ambassadors we are to proclaim the correct evangel; pleading with mankind to be reconciled to God (2 Corinthians 5:18-21). But many within Christianity today spend all of their time preaching Old Testament wrath, warnings of eternal torment, observance of the law, and multitudes of teachings that are not intended for this present era. We mix the law and grace and distort the truth. Thousands of different churches teach thousands of different and contrary things, breeding confusion.

Satan, the Deceiver, has done a good job of hiding the truth that is so clear in the Scriptures. Orthodoxy is often his instrument for hiding the truth and breeding confusion. But rejoice; because ...

It is God's will that all mankind be saved and come to a realization of the truth, and nothing can prevent that from happening.

Milestones in Paul's Ministry *(The Pause)*

> ## Trail Marker #83
> ## Church structure (3:1)

First we see the qualifications for supervisors within the ecclesia ...
- ✓ *Irreprehensible*
- ✓ *The husband of one wife*
- ✓ *Sober*
- ✓ *Sane*
- ✓ *Decorous (of good behavior)*
- ✓ *Hospitable*
- ✓ *Apt to teach*
- ✓ *No toper (given to wine)*
- ✓ *Not quarrelsome, but lenient*
- ✓ *Pacific*
- ✓ *Not fond of money*
- ✓ *Controlling his own household ideally*
- ✓ *Having his children in subjection with all gravity*
- ✓ *No novice (which would make the person more prone to conceit)*
- ✓ *Having an ideal testimony*

Servants are to be:
- ✓ *Grave*
- ✓ *Not double-tongued*
- ✓ *Not addicted to much wine*
- ✓ *Not avaricious (greedy)*
- ✓ *Having faith with a clear conscience*
- ✓ *Tested*
- ✓ *Their wives also to be grave, not adversaries, sober, faithful*
- ✓ *Husbands of one wife*
- ✓ *Controlling children and their own households ideally*

The organized church in our present day has built an intricate system of bureaucracy which seems quite different from the ecclesia's simplicity as found in the Scriptures. While there is certainly some structure to the ecclesia, leadership seems to be far less formal than the present-day world of bishops, archbishops and popes.

And even within most Protestant denominations or independent churches, great power is often vested in the clergy.

But in Paul's day we see a loosely bound ecclesia that simply recognized elders (those more mature in the faith), supervisors (from the Greek episkopos, and often translated bishop in English translations today), and servants (from the Greek diakonos, and often translated deacon).

And those in Paul's day that did assume a leadership role had certain qualifications.

> Trail Marker #84
> ## The Saviour of ALL mankind (4:10)

God, Who is the Saviour of all mankind, especially of believers.

Many Bible teachers claim that God is the Saviour of all mankind, but this is only effectual for those who believe in this lifetime. But the word here is ESPECIALLY, not exclusively.

God is the Saviour of all mankind, and in a SPECIAL way this affects believers. We who believe can realize and enjoy the expectation we have for things to come once this life has ended, while those who do not believe do not enjoy that assurance. We who believe know that we will live in the eons to come, after the resurrection and snatching away of believers into heaven as promised in 1 Thessalonians 4:13 and following.

Some will not experience life in the eons to come. But nothing will prevent God from ultimately becoming the Saviour of all mankind at the end of the eons, as expressed in 1 Corinthians 15:20-28. Remember, it is God's will that ALL mankind be saved and come to a realization of the truth (2:4). Nothing can prevent that from happening.

> Trail Marker #85
> ## Sound words & teaching (6:3)

If anyone is teaching differently and is not approaching with sound words, <u>even those of our Lord Jesus Christ</u>, and the teaching in accord with devoutness, he is conceited, versed in nothing, but morbid about questionings and controversies, out of which is coming envy, strife, calumnies, wicked suspicions, altercations of men of a decadent mind and deprived of the truth.

Here is a caution for those who are teaching. Are we seeing controversies? Envy? Strife? Let us check ourselves to be sure our teachings are correct.

And note that it is possible to use even the words of our Lord incorrectly. This would seem to imply that the words of Jesus from His earthly ministry may not always apply in all situations in all eras.

I believe this is what is meant by correctly cut or rightly divide the Word of God (2 Timothy 2:15). Always consider the context and what group of people are being addressed by the words of Scripture. We cannot assume, for example, that which was spoken to Israel in a particular era applies to believers in our present era.

> ### Trail Marker #86
> ### Vivifying all – in its own eras (6:13-15)

God, Who is vivifying all ...

Keep this precept unspotted, irreprehensible, unto the advent of our Lord, Christ Jesus, which, to its own eras, the happy and only Potentate will be showing.

To <u>vivify</u> is to make alive. God is vivifying <u>all</u>. He will be showing His plan to each "<u>in its own era</u>."

All are not vivified at the same time, nor is the knowledge of this precept (vivification of all) made known to all at the same time; but in its own eras.

> Trail Marker #87
>
> ## Immortal souls? (6:16)

He is King of kings and Lord of lords, Who alone has immortality.

HE ALONE HAS IMMORTALITY!

The common belief that the human soul is immortal comes from Greek philosophy. Here we see the Scriptures clearly teaching that only Christ has immortality. It will only be at the resurrection that we put on immortality (1 Corinthians 15:54).

When we die we will cease to have any form of life and will lie in the grave totally dependent upon God to resurrect us, as Christ Himself laid in the grave totally dependent upon God to do so. Yet we die with the assurance that God promises to do just that; to resurrect us at some future point when we will put on immortality.

2 Timothy

Milestones in Paul's Ministry *(The Pause)*

> Trail Marker #88
> ## Called before times eonian (1:9)

[God] saves us and calls us with a holy calling, not in accord with our acts, but in accord with His own purpose and the grace which is given to us in Christ Jesus <u>before times eonian</u>, yet now is being manifested through the advent of our Saviour, Christ Jesus, Who, indeed, abolishes death, yet illuminates life and incorruption through the evangel of which I was appointed a herald and an apostle and a teacher of the nations.

Observe three things from this passage.

First; our position in the Body of Christ, and even our salvation (the fact that we are in the Body of Christ at all) is an appointment of God that has nothing to do with our acts or behavior. It is a selection made by God in accord with His purposes and His grace. Whatever gifts we may have, they come from God and we have nothing to boast about.

Second; God's purposes were formulated before the eonian times we read about in the Scriptures; before the dawn of mankind. God is not developing His plan along the way.

Third; God's calling of the Body of Christ, while purposed before times eonian, was not revealed or manifested until Paul's day, through the advent of Christ Jesus and the proclamation of Paul's evangel. This, then, is the purpose of proclaiming the evangel (at least in part); to make manifest the calling of the ecclesia; the Body of Christ.

> ### Trail Marker #89
> ### A pattern of sounds words (1:13)

Have a pattern of sound words, which you hear from me.

It is one thing to quote from or teach from the Scriptures. It is quite another to have a pattern of soundness when handling the Scriptures.

We must take care in our handling of the Scriptures so as not to incorporate pre-conceived biases that might influence our understanding. Even orthodoxy and the organized church may be wrong in its understanding, so we must escape those biases and seek truth directly from a sound handling of the Scriptures.

Perhaps Miles Coverdale said it best in the Preface to the 16th Century version of the Bible; "It shall greatly help ye to understand Scripture if thou mark not only what is spoken or written but: To whom, and by whom; With what words, and at what time; Where, and to what intent; With what circumstance; Considering what goeth before and what followeth."

Milestones in Paul's Ministry *(The Pause)*

> ### Trail Marker #90
> ## All had turned away (1:14-15)

The ideal thing committed to you, guard through the holy spirit which is making its home in us.

Timothy's charge is to guard the truth in the face of false teachings. And we see that the holy spirit; God's spirit; is making its home in "us."

Of this you are aware, that all those in the province of Asia were turned from me, of whom are Phygellus and Hermogenes.

ALL WERE TURNED AWAY!

This passage should shock us! Is not Paul considered the missionary apostle, who took Christianity to the nations; planting and nurturing churches? Is it not the understanding of modern-day Christianity that Paul's work continued to flourish and grow into the churches of our day?

Yet we see here that Paul's work took a huge step back near the end of his life and ministry. There was an apostasy; a falling away. All in Asia had turned from him and from the truth he taught.

Looking again at 1:13, when Paul said: *Have a pattern of sound words, which you hear from me;* we see that as the majority turned away from Paul they were turning away from the sound words proclaimed by Paul.

More on this topic from 2 Timothy 2:17-18 ...

Hymeneus and Philetus, who swerve as to truth, saying the resurrection has already occurred, and are subverting the faith of some.

A focus away from the truth and profane prattling has led these two believers to a misunderstanding, and they now lead others astray. When we hear speculation instead of a focus on what the Scriptures are actually saying, we should take heed of this warning.

Consider for a moment the specific error of Hymeneus and Philetus. They had reached the conclusion that the resurrection had already occurred. Has not much of the organized church fallen into the same error?

The common teaching is that at the time of death the believer is immediately alive in the presence of the Lord. How, then, will that person (already living) be resurrected at some future time? Is this not the same as those in Paul's day who taught that the resurrection had already come?

With all of this in mind ... at what point did the organized church recover from this setback? At what point following Paul's life did the majority of believers finally get it right and stand for the truth.

In Paul's day truth is apparently in the hands of the minority, like Timothy and a select few; with the majority having turned from the truth. I would contend that since Paul's day the organized church has continued in apostasy from the truth.

Yes, there are believers that can be found in the pews of churches around the world; but the preachers, teachers, scholars, authors and other leaders within the organized church cannot be trusted for understanding and teaching the truth.

We are on our own. We cannot trust the organized church that is in apostasy from the truth, regardless of the denomination. *All those in the province of Asia were turned from me.* We must seek truth from the Scriptures, properly and carefully handled, with a focus on having a pattern of sound words.

> Trail Marker #91
> ## Commit truth to faithful men (2:2)

What things you hear from me through many witnesses, these commit to faithful men, who shall be competent to teach others also.

Those within most of the ecclesias (churches) had turned away from Paul. How, then, can the truth be preserved?

Here, late in Paul's ministry, we do not see an organized church structure comprised of elders and deacons, or the bishops and pastors of our present day. Truth was to be preserved by *faithful men* identified by Timothy who could then teach the truth to others.

Speak of these things and entreat and expose with every injunction. (Titus 2:15)

We cannot remain silent when false teaching takes place within the ecclesia. We must speak the truth and expose any false teaching.

DOCTRINE AND BEHAVIOR ARE IMPORTANT!

It seems there are those within the Body of Christ that emphasize behavior at the expense of sound doctrine, and there are those that emphasize sound doctrine at the expense of courteous behavior motivated by love. But to Paul, BOTH are important.

Milestones in Paul's Ministry *(The Pause)*

> Trail Marker #92
> ## Avoid controversy (2:14)

Of these things be reminding them; not to engage in controversy for nothing useful, to the upsetting of those who are hearing.

Finding ones-self in the midst of controversy may be unavoidable at times for the sake of the truth. Even Paul found this to be the case. But let us be sure these occasions are not for *nothing useful* (i.e. insignificant issues).

Later, Paul would write to Timothy:

Stupid and crude questionings refuse, being aware that they are generating fighting. (2 Timothy 2:23)

Now a slave of the Lord must not be fighting, but be gentle toward all, apt to teach, bearing with evil, with meekness training those who are antagonizing, seeing whether God may be giving them repentance to come into a realization of the truth, and they will be sobering up out of the trap of the Adversary. (2 Timothy 2:24)

Timothy is charged, then, to teach with gentleness and meekness those who are antagonizing, to see if God will give them repentance.

> ### Trail Marker #93
> ### Correctly cut the word (2:15)

Endeavor to present yourself to God qualified, an unashamed worker, correctly cutting the word of truth.

This goes beyond memorizing Scripture and applying it in superficial ways, ignoring the context. It is to know in which situations a Scriptural reference applies, and when it does not.

As an example, to correctly cut the word of truth means we cannot take a Scripture directed to Israel and assume that it applies to the Body of Christ. It may have been a word intended for a particular group of people at a particular point in time.

<u>Correctly cut</u> or <u>rightly divide</u> the word of truth. This is Paul's directive to Timothy.

This is Paul's last letter. He knew of the danger of carrying over things from a past dispensation which did not belong in the new dispensation.

There were those clinging to the Law, and to the primacy of Israel. But these were things from a past era. God was doing a new thing; Israel having been set aside for a season. Israel is no longer in a seat of preference.

The Body of Christ, as revealed by God thru Paul, was comprised of Jew and Gentile with no barrier or preference. To reach into the past and to carry over truths from that previous era would contaminate or confuse the truth that God now wanted to reveal. Paul knew the danger of this as his life neared its end, and here in his last letter he saw the need to warn Timothy. The truth as found in all of God's revelation must be RIGHTLY DIVIDED!

Milestones in Paul's Ministry *(The Pause)*

> ### Trail Marker #94
> # Wickedness will grow (3:1)

Now this know, that in the last days perilous periods will be present, for men will be selfish, fond of money, ostentatious, proud, calumniators, stubborn to parents, ungrateful, malign, without natural affection, implacable, adversaries, uncontrollable, fierce, averse to the good, traitors, rash, conceited, fond of their own gratification rather than fond of God ...

Are we in the last days today? This seems to be an apt description of our current society. But read on ...

Having a form of devoutness yet denying its power.

This, then, speaks not of society; but of organized religion. There is a *form of devoutness* (reverence of God), but it is only form and not substance. It is the organized church (religion) that will grow in wickedness in the "last days" described by Paul.

Shun false teachers. (3:5)

They slip into homes. They are led by lusts and gratifications. They are always learning but never come into a realization of the truth. They are like Jannes and Jambres who opposed Moses, withstanding the truth; men of a depraved mind, disqualified as to the faith. But they shall not be progressing more, for their folly shall be obvious to all.

Just as Jannes and Jambres were exposed and thwarted, so also will every false teacher, as God is in control.

Wicked men and swindlers shall wax worse and worse, deceiving and being deceived. (3:13)

Milestones in Paul's Ministry *(The Pause)*

> **Trail Marker #95**
>
> **All scripture is inspired** (3:15-17)

The sacred scriptures are able to make you wise for salvation through faith which is in Christ Jesus. All scripture is inspired by God, and is beneficial for teaching, for exposure, for correction, for discipline in righteousness, that the man of God may be equipped, fitted out for every good act.

While all Scripture is inspired by God and beneficial for these purposes, this does not mean that all Scripture can be applied to all situations in all eras.

We remember Pauls' words elsewhere in this same letter. *Have a pattern of sound words* (1:13). *Endeavor to present yourself to God qualified, an unashamed worker, correctly cutting the word of truth* (2:15).

Milestones in Paul's Ministry *(The Pause)*

> Trail Marker #96
> ## The falling away (4:3)

For the era will be when they will not tolerate sound teaching, but, their hearing being tickled, they will heap up for themselves teachers in accord with their own desires, and, indeed, they will be turning their hearing away from the truth yet will be turned aside to myths.

Could this be a description of Christianity today, with so many flocking to dumbed-down, easy-to-read Bible translations and popular authors and Bible teachers; to have their hearing tickled?

Paul's death is imminent. (4:6)

For I am already a libation, and the period of my dissolution is imminent. I have contended the ideal contest. I have finished my career. I have kept the faith.

Here we see the reason Paul is preparing Timothy to carry on his work. His death is imminent.

Note that at the end of Paul's life the "church" is turning away from the truth; seeking teachers who teach in accord with their own desires. Does this not describe the organized church today?

If one hears a word he does not like, he simply moves on to a different church preaching a message that is more appealing. Can we not see that many different churches preaching conflicting messages breeds confusion? How can one find the truth? Only through a study of the Scriptures, and not through the teachings and doctrines of the majority (i.e. the organized church).

Paul beckons for help to come quickly. (4:9)

Endeavor to come to me quickly, for Demas, loving the current eon, forsook me and went to Thessalonica, Crescens to Galatia, Titus to Dalmatia. Luke only is with me. Lead Mark back with you, for he is useful to me for service. When you come, bring the traveling cloak which I left in Troas with Carpus, and the scrolls, especially the vellums. Alexander the coppersmith displayed to me

Milestones in Paul's Ministry *(The Pause)*

much evil: the Lord will be paying him in accord with his acts. Very much he withstood our words.

Those forsaking Paul were loving the current eon more than the evangel and the things of God.

Timothy is asked to bring with him Mark, and to bring the travelling cloak which Paul left in Troas with Carpus, and the scrolls, especially the vellums.

Travelling cloak (*phelanes* in the Greek, or *bark*) could be a reference to a covering for the scrolls and vellums; writings Paul wished to preserve knowing his death was imminent and knowing that the majority were already turning away from correct doctrine. How could truth be preserved after Paul's death? (This is the only time *phelanes* is used and is translated *valise* in the Syriac version.)

Ernest Martin, in his book, *The Original Bible Restored,* argues that when Paul wrote to Timothy his primary goal was that sound doctrine be preserved after his death. Therefore it was necessary for the apostles to leave behind an official documentation of truth.

It would not make sense that the apostles would simply die and allow "church leaders" to set Scriptural standards. If they couldn't trust the doctrines of many in their midst while they still lived, how could they depend on them to preserve correct doctrine in the future?

We know that many in Paul's day were writing "gospels" (Luke 1:1 and note the many publications in our present day that purport to be "lost scriptures"). There was a danger of losing the truth altogether if the apostles did not act to leave behind some official documentation.

Martin notes that Paul wanted John Mark, the author of the Gospel of Mark, to come with Timothy to perform a "service." John Mark was at times an associate of Paul, but he was more closely tied to Peter who refers to him as "my son" (1 Peter 5:13).

When asking Timothy to bring Mark, he also asks him to bring the traveling cloak *which I left in Troas with Carpus, and the scrolls, especially the vellums* (4:13). Cloak could refer to a receptacle for the scrolls and vellums (or parchments), much like the cover for a book, or a case.

Martin hypothesizes that knowing his death was approaching, Paul asks Timothy and Mark to come to Rome with certain specific writings (the scrolls and vellums), and the "service" Paul intended for Mark was perhaps to take Paul's inspired writings to Peter for inclusion in the Scriptural canon.

In light of the apostasy growing within the ecclesia, Paul's impending death, and his concern for the preservation of truth, Martin's hypothesis seems to make great sense. And while we cannot be sure that Martin is correct on all counts, one thing is certain; Paul sees the preservation of correct doctrine as essential.

Paul goes on.

At my first defense no one came along with me, but all forsook me. (4:16)

Again we see that near the end of Paul's life the majority had turned from him. This should cause us to question the "truth" being taught by the majority (i.e. the organized church in its variety of denominations and sects). At what point in history, following Paul's death, did the majority suddenly reverse its apostasy and error and find the truth?

Milestones in Paul's Ministry *(The Pause)*

> ### Trail Marker #97
> ## No greetings to the ecclesias (4:19)

Greet Prisca, Aquila and the household of Onesiphorus. Endeavor to come before winter. Greeting you is Eubulus, Pudens, Linus, Claudia and all the brethren.

It is interesting that here, near the end of Paul's life, he no longer sends greeting to or from the ecclesia at various places. Instead his greetings refer to individuals. This shows the growing informality of the ecclesia, or church, and the fact that the truth is in the hands of individuals who had not turned away.

Charles Welch (Christian theologian and writer 1888-1967) observed that 2 Timothy reveals a church in ruins, and the discipline that was possible when the church was intact was no longer effective. So Timothy is instructed to exercise discipline upon himself, not upon others (2:19; 3:5).

Beware of the organized church. Seeks truth from the Scriptures, questioning doctrine being taught by the majority. Remember that even in Paul's day, near the end of his life, the majority had rejected the truth and were in apostasy.

> Trail Marker #98
> ## The difference between 1 & 2 Timothy

2 Timothy is perhaps Paul's final letter. His career was finished (4:7). The ecclesia had become filled with evil. And Paul's basic instruction is to separate from evil.

Consider the change that had taken place since Paul's first letter to Timothy. In 1 Timothy there were false teachers in the ecclesia (1:3-7) but Paul still emphasized the leadership to be provided by supervisors and servants; "bishops" and "deacons" in the Authorized Version. Paul warned that in latter times some would depart from the faith (4:1). But elders that ruled well were to be honored (5:17).

But in 2 Timothy we hear that all in Asia had turned away (1:15). Orderly rule is now succeeded by ruin. Instead of mentioning supervisors, servants or elders within the ecclesia, Timothy is instructed to commit the truth to "faithful men" (2:2). Paul's instruction is simply to preach the truth, and to commit truth to faithful men who would be able to teach others. There is no longer any talk of organization within the ecclesia; for the ecclesia is now in ruin. And worse things were to come in the last days.

The ecclesia had departed from truth. Leaders such as Hymenaeus and Philetus were leading some astray, teaching that the resurrection had already occurred (2:18). Whereas 1 Timothy provided characteristics to be found within supervisor and servants who would lead the ecclesia, in 2 Timothy we simply read that a servant of the Lord was to be gentle and meek (2:24). Deceit and apostasy within the ecclesia were growing. In the last days, perilous times were to come (3:1). There would be a form of godliness that denied the power (3:5). Evil men would grow worse; and this referred to men within the ecclesia who would be deceiving and being deceived (3:13). The time would come when *they* (those within the ecclesia) would not endure sound doctrine (4:3). Demas, Crescens and Titus forsook Paul, preferring the present world (4:10).

And so we note the transition between a somewhat organized structure within the ecclesia in 1 Timothy; with an emphasis on supervisors and servants (bishops and deacons); and the absence of structure in 2 Timothy where we see an emphasis on the individual servant of the Lord, and committing the truth to faithful men. And in the midst of this growing apostasy within the ecclesia; even within the leadership of the ecclesia; Paul knew his death was drawing near (4:6). So he makes provision for Timothy and Mark to gather his writings and to bring them to him, where he would make arrangements for these writings to be preserved after his death, in order that the truth might be preserved in the midst of growing apostasy (4:12).

With all of this in mind, does it not cause us to question the teachings propagated by the leaders within the organized church today? At what point following Paul's death did the apostasy cease? At what point was spiritual truth, as proclaimed by Paul, finally recognized and taught by the majority within the church?

Titus

> **Trail Marker #99**
> ## God's progressive revelation (1:1-3)

... a realization of the truth, which accords with devoutness, in expectation of life eonian, yet manifests His word <u>in its own eras</u> by heralding, with which I was entrusted.

The realization of eonian life (life in the eons to come) is made known by proclaiming the evangel, and it is manifested *in its own eras,* or progressively.

To Israel the prophets had foretold an eventual restoration of the kingdom and a resurrection for life upon the earth. But it was not until the revelation given to Paul that we learn of the Body of Christ and its destiny in the heavens in the ages to come. God's truth is manifested progressively, in its own eras.

If God's revelation is progressive, we see the great importance of "rightly dividing" the Word; else we run the risk of applying statements and situations to our current situation when they were, in fact, intended for a previous era.

Milestones in Paul's Ministry *(The Pause)*

> Trail Marker #100
> ## Preserve sound faith ^(1:10)

Many are insubordinate, vain praters and imposters, especially those of the Circumcision, who must be gagged, who are subverting whole households, teaching what they must not, on behalf of sordid gain.

Be exposing them severely, <u>that they may be sound in the faith</u>, not heeding Jewish myths and precepts of men who are turning them from the truth.

All is clean to the clean, but to the defiled and unbelieving nothing is clean, but their mind as well as conscience is defiled. They are avowing an acquaintance with God, yet by their acts are denying it, being abominable and stubborn, and disqualified for every good act.

There were problems to be addressed at Crete, especially among the Circumcision.

> Trail Marker #101
> ## Saving grace to all humanity (2:11)

For the saving grace of God made its advent to all humanity ...

Consistent with so many other passages in the Scriptures that are often limited and restricted to SOME, Paul here notes to Timothy that God's saving grace has come to ALL humanity.

Milestones in Paul's Ministry *(The Pause)*

> Trail Marker #102
> ## Respond with ideal acts (2:12)

God's saving grace is training us that, disowning irreverence and worldly desires, we should be <u>living sanely</u> and <u>justly</u> and <u>devoutly</u> in the current eon, anticipating that happy expectation, the advent of the glory of the great God and our Saviour, Jesus Christ, Who gives Himself for us, that He should be redeeming us from all lawlessness and be cleansing for Himself a people to be about Him, <u>zealous of ideal acts</u>.

God's glory is not yet evident in this present eon, but we know it is coming and can therefore "expect" it and bask in that happy expectation.

As for this call to be zealous of ideal acts; salvation is not dependent upon acts as it is entirely a gracious gift from God. But in response to that gift we should seek to exhibit ideal acts.

Paul instructs Timothy to remind them of proper behavior. (3:1)
- ✓ To be subject to sovereignties and authorities
- ✓ To be yielding
- ✓ To be ready for every good work
- ✓ To be calumniating (**speaking badly of**) no one
- ✓ To be pacific
- ✓ To be lenient
- ✓ To display meekness toward all humanity

Why is this important?

Because we also were once foolish, stubborn, deceived, slaves of various desires and gratifications, malicious, envious, detestable and hateful.

But when our Saviour's kindness and fondness for humanity made its advent, not according to works but according to His mercy, He saves and renews us, justifies us in His grace, and makes us enjoyers in expectation of the allotment of life eonian.

<u>Insist that believers exhibit ideal acts</u> (3:8)

Insist that those who have believed God may be concerned to preside for ideal acts, for this is ideal and beneficial for humanity. Stand aloof from stupid questionings, genealogies, strifes and fightings about law; as they are of no benefit.

Again; salvation is not dependent on works, or ideal acts. But Paul continually stresses the importance of works within the ecclesia.

Turn out the sectarian man (3:10)

After warning a sectarian man a second time, refuse him. He has turned himself out and is sinning and self-condemned.

Philemon

> **Trail Marker #103**
> ## The ecclesia at your house (1:2)

Notice the simplicity of church structure in the statement, *The ecclesia at your house*. Unlike the "First Church of XYZ" of our day or the multitudes of denominations and organizational hierarchies, here we see the simplicity of a church, or ecclesia (called-out-ones) at the house of a believer.

And let us not make the assumption that there is a regular, weekly assembly at this house. Paul seems to be simply greeting those who are a part of the ecclesia (the called-out-ones) that reside at this house.

Milestones in Paul's Ministry *(The Pause)*

> Trail Marker #104
> ## Entreaty for Onesimus (1:10-14)

I entreat you concerning Onesimus, whom I sent back to you. I had intended to keep him for myself, to serve me in the bonds of the evangel. But apart from your opinion I want to do nothing, that your good may not be as of compulsion but voluntary.

Paul would like Philemon to give Onesimus his release from slavery, allowing him to serve Paul in the bonds of the evangel. Yet Paul is sending back Onesimus (who had obviously fled) to Philemon, hoping he will be released voluntarily.

Paul notes that the release of Onesiumus would be proper, but because of love he *entreats* rather than compels.

Milestones in Paul's Ministry *(The Pause)*

> Trail Marker #105
> ## Summary of Paul's ministry

As we conclude our journey through Paul's life and letters, and as we prepare to look at Revelation, let's recap a few things.

First; Paul is the only voice found in the New Testament that is directed to the nations ... those who are outside of the people of Israel. On the road to Damascus he received a dual commission: *He is a choice instrument of Mine, to bear My name before both the nations and kings, besides the sons of Israel* (Acts 9:15-16). Peter, John, James and other New Testament writers had a commission to Israel *only*. Paul <u>alone</u> was commissioned to go to the Gentiles.

As Paul went to the Gentiles his message was not the same as the message proclaimed to the believers of Israel by the others. Paul stressed that the gospel he proclaimed was not received from man, but it came through a revelation of Jesus Christ (Galatians 1:11-12). If he preached the same gospel, why would he not have studied under the Twelve who had heard and observed Christ during His earthly ministry? And why would Paul refer to his proclamation as "<u>my</u> evangel" instead of "<u>the</u> evangel" (Romans 2:16; 16:25-26)?

Paul had been entrusted with the evangel of the Uncircumcision, and Peter had been trusted with the evangel of the Circumcision (Galatians 2:7). He did not say that his was the evangel *to* the Uncircumcision; but *of* the Uncircumcision. It was a <u>*different*</u> message.

Paul tells us that at some point Israel had been temporarily set aside: *Callousness, in part, on Israel has come UNTIL the complement of the nations may be entering* (Romans 11:25). So Israel, which had long been God's chosen instrument through which He worked, was set aside. But this setting aside is not permanent, but only UNTIL!

Now as Paul proclaimed God's grace and freedom from the law, he noted there will come a day of indignation. But *God did not appoint us* [the Body of Christ] *to indignation* (1 Thessalonians 5:8). We will read of this "day of indignation;" the Day of the Lord; in Revelation. But since the Body of Christ was not appointed to indignation, how will God bring this about upon the earth?

There will come a day when the Body of Christ is "snatched away" (1 Thessalonians 4:13) to serve Christ in the celestials (Ephesians 2:6). This must occur so that the day of indignation (Romans 2:5) can come upon the earth, without subjecting the Body of Christ to this indignation. And this removal is necessary, since the man of lawlessness (the antichrist) cannot be revealed until "the detainer" (2 Thessalonians 2:6) is removed.

And so we will notice when studying Revelation that the Body of Christ is not to be found, for the Body has been "snatched away" from the earth before the events of Revelation (God's indignation) unfold. With this in mind let us now turn to the final book in God's Word; Revelation.

Milestones in Paul's Ministry *(The Pause)*

Milestones in Revelation
"The Return of the King"

An Overview of the Scriptures, by
BOB EVELY © 2018.
An Independent Minister of Christ Jesus,
Of the church at Wilmore, Kentucky

E. W. Bullinger says this about Bible study within today's church: "No matter what part of the Bible may be read, the one object seems to be to find the Church. For, the Word of truth not being rightly divided, or indeed divided at all, the whole Bible is supposed to be about every one, in every part, and in every age; and the Church is supposed to be its one pervading subject."

By carelessly, or at times purposefully, combining all things revealed in Scripture without observing to whom or in what age a word pertains makes it *impossible* to discern what God is revealing to us. God may be revealing a certain truth that pertained to *Israel*, and perhaps only for a particular period of time. Yet the church today will often substitute *the church* for Israel, claiming something for ourselves that does not pertain to us at all. Thus, that which God has revealed to us is lost or distorted.

If care is taken in our handling of the truths found in Revelation, we will see that **it does not pertain to the church** (the Body of Christ) at all. Its subject is God's dealings with ISRAEL, and with the Gentile nations, in a time AFTER the Body of Christ has been removed from the earth.

As we walk thru Revelation, observe that the Body of Christ is not found anywhere in the book!

Again turning to Bullinger, who observes the following concerning the book of Revelation: "It is not only Hebrew in character as to its linguistic peculiarities, but especially in its use of the Old Testament. ... All who know anything of Old Testament history cannot fail to detect the almost constant reference to it."

How does Revelation fit-in with the remainder of the Bible?

God's Word is progressive and unfolding. God began with creation, and selected certain individuals thru whom He would speak ... Abraham, Isaac, Jacob (Israel), and then the people of Israel. So God moved from working thru select individuals to working thru an entire nation; Israel. But even then, it was His intent to bless all the peoples of the earth; all nations; thru Israel. (See Genesis 12:3; 22:18; 26:4-5; 28:14)

When Israel began to go astray God chose prophets to speak to the nation and to call her back to repentance and obedience. But continued rebellion led to exile. Still the prophets spoke and promised a restoration of the kingdom that had once been established by David. The people awaited this restoration and the promised Messiah who would bring the restoration.

In the gospel accounts the Messiah (Christ) comes, speaking of the nearness of the kingdom. This was the promise the people had been waiting for. But Christ was rejected by Israel, and as a result there was a delay in the kingdom's restoration. But in Acts the Twelve carry on with the same message. If the people would repent, Christ would return and there would be a restoration of the kingdom. (Acts 3:19-21) But still the people rejected Christ (Acts 28:26-28), and the kingdom was further delayed.

So, God did a new thing; an amazing thing. Setting aside Israel *temporarily* (Romans 11:25) He spoke directly to the nations thru a new apostle; Paul. Paul was not one of the Twelve, but was an ADDITIONAL apostle with a new mission, unheard of in the past. He would speak to the nations, introducing the Body of Christ consisting of Jew and Gentile alike with no barrier or preference. This created no small stir, for Israel was offended by this heretical message. (Acts 22:21-23) THEY were the people of God, not the nations.

While Paul proclaimed the message assigned to him (the evangel of the Uncircumcision per Galatians 2:7), Peter and the others continued with their message to Israel ... repent and the kingdom would be restored. Peter and the other Circumcision writers penned their letters to the Circumcision as they awaited the kingdom. Repent, have faith and good works, and persevere! Israel still awaited the kingdom's restoration. And Revelation is the fulfillment of what they waited for. Christ, the King, returns; the kingdom is established once again; and faithful Israel serves its place as Christ rules over all the nations.

But what happened to the Body of Christ?

Israel is mentioned time and again throughout Revelation, but whenever the nations are mentioned it is always negative. It is Israel as contrasted with the nations. Nowhere do we see "the church" or the Body of Christ. This shows us that somewhere along the way the Body of Christ was removed from the scene in order that the turbulent times could proceed, and Satan could lead the ultimate rebellion without being impeded by the Body of Christ or the holy spirit that filled them.

We see this "removal" in 1 Thessalonians 4 when Christ sounds the trump, the dead in Christ rise, and the living in Christ rise to meet Him in the air.

And the Body of Christ begins its commission of reigning in the heavens, for its expectation was always related to the celestials and not the earth. And then, sometime after this, Christ returns to the earth and restores the kingdom with faithful Israel reigning with Him.

The Body of Christ reigning in the heavens, and Israel reigning upon the earth, we enter the final phase of God's restoration process. All of life to this point has been a process, but now we get closer and closer to the final goal. Paul records this in 1 Corinthians 15 where we see death abolished, all subjected to Christ, and God becoming All in all.

So as we study Revelation we must remember its context. While it may be positioned as the final book in the Bible, it does not reveal to us the "final condition" of mankind. At the end of the book the process continues, and only in Paul's writings are we told of the conclusion; the consummation.

Today we live in an era of grace as revealed to us by the apostle Paul. God is conciliated to the world, not reckoning mankind's offenses to them. (2 Corinthians 5:19) But a day will come when God will take the next step in His plan to reconcile all to Himself. Grace will not reign in that future era, but judgment; for judgment is what it will take to bring the most stubborn and rebellious into the fold.

In that future era Christ's ambassadors (2 Corinthians 5:20) will be *recalled*, as is typically the case when conditions become perilous in the nations where ambassadors serve. War is about to be declared on the rebellious world.

Even today mankind seems to have not only forgotten God, but has lost all consciousness to His existence. He is shut out of their every thought. And in the future era described in Revelation, this will be true to the extreme!

The world wants peace and satisfaction *without* Christ. And while the world will not respond to Christ, they will receive the antichrist. Using Satan, God will send to mankind a strong deception that they should believe the lie. God wants mankind to acknowledge Him and the supremacy of His spirit. For some, the events described in Revelation are necessary to lead mankind to this conclusion. And so the bulk of this book records the waging of a brief but decisive war by God to recover a lost world.

The world today is filled with plans to redeem mankind. Peace conferences are planned with great hope. Democracy is promoted as the great deliverer of mankind. Band together all nations into one and wars will cease. But democracy is inadequate. Dictators, even the most charismatic and well-intentioned, are inadequate. No one is able! It is God's intention that man come to this realization and turn to Him; but throughout Revelation in the final ages upon this earth we see a rebellious mankind turn to any scheme or person other than God to accomplish peace and satisfaction without Him.

A brief word on the differing interpretations of Revelation

When it comes to prophecy, and especially the book of Revelation, there are a number of distinct, broad interpretations. G.K. Chesterton commented in *Orthodoxy*, *"Though St. John the Evangelist saw many strange monsters in his vision, he saw no creatures so wild as one of his own commentators."*

Years ago Jill and I participated in a couples Bible Study group, and at one point we decided to study Revelation. We thought a good approach might be to have each couple purchase a different commentary on the book, and as we discussed each chapter each could share thoughts from the commentary they had chosen. It didn't take long for us to see that interpretations and opinions were widely varied. Some believed the events of Revelation had already taken place in full. Others taught that these events would occur in the future. And as for the details of every part of Revelation, there was great disagreement. Yet each of these commentaries spoke with authority. While differing interpretations can be found for every part of the Bible, it is especially prevalent with Revelation.

My comments will represent my own current understanding, based on my studies. As always, I encourage you to study the Scriptures and to think for yourself. Think about what others (including myself) are saying, but never think any person is the authority. All human beings are fallible.

But let me say this. Regardless of one's interpretation of this book, our daily walk should not be affected. Some will say that those awaiting the Lord to come and snatch them away ("the rapture") are poor stewards of God's creation in this present world. This should not be the case. Paul, the apostle to the nations, always encouraged his audience to live a life worthy of their calling, and to work for the good of all. This is our mandate regardless of how we see the events of Revelation unfolding, past or future.

So now ... let us begin our walk thru ...

REVELATION

REVELATION
The Return of the King

As we begin our walk thru Revelation, let us recall these words from the apostle Paul ... *be learning not to be disposed above what is written.* (1 Corinthians 4:6)

More than any other portion of God's Word, Revelation is the subject of great speculation. Many different authors, scholars, and teachers will tell us what every detail means. But since there is much disagreement among them, we should proceed with care. Let us consider that which is *revealed* to us, without speculating on those things which the Lord saw fit to leave less obvious.

> ## Trail Marker #1
> ## The "Unveiling" (1:1)

The <u>unveiling of Jesus Christ</u>, which God gives to Him, to show to His slaves what must occur swiftly; and He signifies it, dispatching through His messenger to His slave John, who testifies ... whatever he perceived.

The King James Version assigns the title, "The Revelation of St. John the Divine." But this is not the revelation or unveiling, of St. John. It is "The Unveiling of Jesus Christ!" It is not a revelation only of things to come, but an unveiling of a person; Jesus Christ! It is a revelation given THRU John, but is an unveiling OF Jesus Christ.

The Greek is *apokalupsis* from which we get our English *apocalypse*. Most translations render the word *revelation*. Things that have been concealed in the past are now *revealed* by God. The Concordant Version renders the word *unveiling*.

To the Believer in this present age, Jesus Christ has been *unveiled*. We recognize Him as Lord; as the Son of God. But to the world He remains veiled, ever since He departed earth and ascended into heaven following the resurrection. Furthermore, even to the Believer the things that are to take place in the future are *veiled* until God provides the *unveiling*. This He has done in His Word.

The book of Revelation records Christ's unveiling as it pertains to His return to the earth to reign. The tribulation to take place prior to Christ's return to the earth, and His long-awaited return, have been revealed to John and are recorded in this book.

We recall that John, the author of Revelation, was one of the Twelve; commissioned to go solely to Israel!

Christ revealed to John that which ISRAEL could expect; for Christ to return to the earth, to restore the kingdom to Israel and to reign. This is what we read about in Revelation.

Revelation is not about the expectation of the Body of Christ; Paul was commissioned to write about that. John is commissioned to write to Israel concerning *her* expectation. Pay close attention, and you will see many references to Israel throughout Revelation ... and <u>no</u> references to the Body of Christ.

Throughout Revelation, John is permitted to *perceive* (to see) certain things; things he has been commanded to record. The book of Revelation is John's report.

So, Jesus Christ, Who had died and was resurrected and ascended into heaven, is now UNVEILED. John has been selected to receive God's revelation.

> ## Trail Marker #2
> ## The era is near ^(1:3)

Happy is he who is reading and those who are hearing the word of the prophecy, and who are keeping that which is written in it, for the era is near.

Near is conditional. Epaphroditus was *near* death, but he recovered. (Philippians 2:30) The Lord proclaimed that the kingdom was *near* during His earthly ministry, but it was not realized in short order because Israel rejected her king.

Furthermore, the era may be *near* in God's timing, but to Him a day may be like a thousand years. (2 Peter 3:8)

Trail Marker #3
The address on the envelope (1:4)

John; to the seven ecclesias which are in the province of Asia.

WARNING: Most Bible translations use "church" for ecclesia throughout Revelation. But the ecclesia (called-out-ones) that John addressed was comprised exclusively of Israelite believers.

John, as one of the Twelve, always addressed the Jewish believers; never the nations. The ecclesias ("called-out-ones") in this case are the believers from among Israel.

And makes us a kingdom and priests to His God and Father, to Him be glory and might for the eons of the eons. (1:6)

To the Jews it was given to be *priests* unto God. *Priests* is not a term ever used of a Gentile, or of the Body of Christ. *Priests* always have to do with Israel.

As we proceed, look closely for the many references to Israel throughout Revelation. The content speaks to and of Israel and not the Body of Christ.

Also note *eons of the eons* in this passage. This makes reference to at least two eons (eons is plural) out of all of the eons (or ages). It is the last two eons that are spoken of here, when Christ reigns upon the earth. Christ will not reign "forever and ever" but only *for the eons of the eons*, UNTIL all is subjected to Him (1 Corinthians 15:25) and He completes the purpose God has assigned to Him, and He turns the kingdom over to the Father.

> Trail Marker #4
> # In the Lord's Day (1:9-10)

I, John ... came to be in the island called Patmos. I came to be, in spirit, in the Lord's day.

John finds himself on the island of Patmos and is caused to be *in spirit* (as contrasted with *in flesh*). John was not in the Spirit "on" the Lord's day. Instead, he found himself "in" the Lord's day.

E. W. Bullinger wrote, "It is not a question of when John received this vision: but of what he saw in it. Whether it was a Sunday or Monday can have no real relation to the book. Our lot is cast in 'Man's day.' (1 Corinthians 4:3) Now is the time when man is judging; and few, if any, escape from experiencing sad proofs of the fact. But, thank God, 'man's day' will not go on forever. Another day is coming, and that will be 'the Lord's Day.' Then, He will be the judge."

Christian orthodoxy has perpetuated the misconception that *the Lord's day* is Sunday, the "Christian sabbath." But the Bible speaks of no such thing as a Christian sabbath. The sabbath, being the seventh day, was given to the Jew to observe as a part of the law.

The problem is that many believers seek to *substitute* themselves for Israel throughout the Scriptures, but there is no Biblical warrant to do so.

In this present age there is no such day designated as *the Lord's day*. This is a fabrication of man's traditions. *The Lord's day* instead refers to a time not yet here, when *man's day* will cease and when *the Lord's day* will begin. To John it was given to experience *the Lord's day* that will occur in the future, enabling him to bring this revelation of Christ to mankind.

There is no difference in meaning between the phrase *the Lord's day* and *the day of the Lord*. The linguistic difference relates only to emphasis. The prophets emphasized the character of *the day* that was to come (the day of the Lord), while John emphasizes *the Lord* as He is unveiled and exalted (the Lord's day). The Scriptures speak often of the day of the Lord.

There are three distinct days mentioned in God's Word. Paul refers to our present day as *man's day* or *the day of man.* (1 Corinthians 4:3) This is a day to which Paul has no desire to conform. Man is judging. During this era man displays what he is not capable of accomplishing on his own. No matter what the circumstance, the form of government (even democracy) or the proliferation of well-intentioned laws, there is continued failure.

Man's day will come to an end when *the day of the Lord* arrives, but it must last long enough to allow humanity to prove its inabilities. Thankfully, man's day will not go on forever.

The day of the Lord, into which John finds himself transported in his vision, is the time foretold by the prophets. In this day the Lord is exalted.

And God will be exalted on the new earth, in *the day of God.* (2 Peter 3:12)

So, to facilitate this revelation given to John, he is temporarily "transported" to this era called *the Lord's day* and he will see and record the events that will take place in that future day. By the spirit John saw the events that will take place in *The Day of the Lord.*

Milestones in Revelation *(Return of the King)*

> Trail Marker #5
>
> ## The seven ecclesias (1:11)

I hear behind me a voice, loud as a trumpet, saying, What you are observing write into a scroll and send it to the seven ecclesias: to Ephesus and to Smyrna and to Pergamum and to Thyatira and to Sardis and to Philadelphia and to Laodicia.

E.W. Bullinger observes that in every part of the Bible the one object for many readers is to find the Church. There is no attempt to *rightly divide* the Word of God in accord with 2 Timothy 2:15. It is assumed that all of the Bible speaks directly to us in our present day and situation. But ...

TODAY'S CHURCH IS NOT THE SUBJECT OF REVELATION.

Instead we see God's final dealings with the Jew and the nations; not the Body of Christ. Throughout we see Jewish imagery; the Temple, the Tabernacle, the Ark of the Covenant, the Altar, the Incense, the Priests. All of this belongs to Israel, not the Body of Christ which is conspicuously absent.

The Body of Christ today is waiting to be received up in glory. (1 Timothy 3:16) We await our calling on high. (Philippians 3:14) We look for Christ to change these mortal bodies into a glorious body like His own. (Philippians 3:20,21) And with the Body of Christ nowhere to be found in Revelation it seems that these things will take place before the opening of Revelation.

There are various theories concerning the seven *ecclesias*, most often translated "churches," to whom these letters are addressed. Some say these are seven different *kinds* of ecclesias that represent the many other ecclesias in that day. Others say these seven ecclesias represent the various kinds of churches, good and bad, in our present day. Or perhaps these are seven specific ecclesias that *will* exist at the opening of the Lord's Day.

Regardless, while we can certainly learn from the letters directed to these seven ecclesias as to behaviors and attitudes that God approves of and that which God does not approve of; we must be careful not to see these letters speaking directly to us in our present day. As we will see, these ecclesias are comprised exclusively of believers from among Israel.

Trail Marker #6
The messengers (1:20)

The secret of the seven stars and the seven lampstands. The seven stars are messengers of the seven ecclesias, and the seven lampstands are seven ecclesias.

Let us recall the lampstand in the Tabernacle in Exodus 25. There we saw one lampstand with seven lamps. But now scattered, Israel is here represented by seven lampstands. As one lampstand represented Israel in unity, seven lampstands represents Israel in dispersion.

A *messenger* (*angelos* in the Greek) can be either an angelic being or a human being. Both can be found in the Scriptures, and only the context can tell us if a messenger is an angel or a human. *Messenger* refers to the being's mission, not its composition.

In the present context we ask; what purpose would there be in directing letters to angels?

Furthermore, within a synagogue there is a *messenger* or legate that ranks directly below the chief of the synagogue. He is the mouthpiece of the congregation. So, it appears that these letters to the seven ecclesias are directed to this mouthpiece of each congregation. And this displays once again that ...

It is ISRAEL, with its synagogues and messengers, that is the focus of Revelation.

> ### Trail Marker #7
> # The letter to the Ephesians (2:1)

Commendations: Acts, toil, endurance, refusal to bear evil men, trying and finding false those saying they are apostles who are not, bearing because of My name and not being wearied, hating the acts of the Nicolaitans which I also hate.

Criticisms: Leaving your first love.

Charge: Remember whence you have fallen, repent, and do the former acts.

Warning: If not I am coming to you and will remove your lampstand.

<u>Compare this letter to the Ephesians with Paul's letter to the Ephesians.</u>

Is there any similarity? Paul's letter is on such a high plane; with spiritual promises and expectations; and rooted purely in grace and not law. Not so with this letter to the Ephesians recorded by John. Why?

I contend that the Body of Christ has been removed from the scene before the events of Revelation begin to unfold. The age of grace has ended. God once again works with and thru Israel, under a covenant of law.

The words *"to him that overcometh"* are foreign to Paul. The Body of Christ has already overcome *in Him*. They are already more than conquerors. But those being addressed here in Revelation are living in the era of the beast, and great tribulation. The call to those living in this future era is to overcome, and to endure to the end.

> **Trail Marker #8**
> ## Those saying they are Jews (2:9)

To the ecclesia in Smyrna ...

You are bearing the calumny of those saying they are Jews but are not; but are a synagogue of Satan.

Observe the reference to those saying they are Jews, and who are obviously speaking poorly (with calumny) of those in the ecclesia who by inference are truly Jews. And observe the reference to *the synagogue of Satan.*

These references show us it is ISRAEL that is being addressed and not the Body of Christ. When has it ever been a requirement to "profess to be Jews" to enter the ecclesia of today; the Body of Christ?

> ### Trail Marker #9
> ## Authority over the nations (2:26)

To the ecclesia in Thyatira ...

To those who are conquering and keeping my acts until the consummation, I will be giving authority over the nations, and he will be shepherding them with an iron club as vessels of pottery are crushed.

Again we see that this message is being directed to ISRAEL.

Those faithful within the Jewish ecclesia (called-out-ones) will have authority over the nations when Christ returns. Israel will serve as Christ's right hand in bringing those of the nations into subjection.

The contrast here is *Israel* and *the nations*. There is no Body of Christ to be seen. Remember, to Paul there was no Jew or Greek ... no preference was given to any nation as Israel had once enjoyed in her past. But now, with the Body of Christ removed from the scene, the faithful among Israel become God's chosen instrument to work thru upon the earth.

A side note ... It is interesting that Tertullian and Epiphanius say there was no ecclesia in Thyatira when John wrote. But remember, John has been "transported" to a future day; *the Day of the Lord;* and in that day there will be an ecclesia at this place.

> ## Trail Marker #10
> ## The scroll of life (3:5)

To the ecclesia in Sardis ...

The one who is conquering shall be clothed in white garments and his name will not be erased from the scroll of life, and I will be avowing his name before My Father and His messengers.

We within the Body of Christ are unworthy in ourselves, but worthy in Christ. But in this future era one will be worthy based on their own merit; their *overcoming* and *remaining faithful* to the end.

The *scroll of life* is mentioned six times in Revelation. It consists of the names of those who do not worship the wild beast (chapters 13 and 17).

The scroll (or book) is also mentioned in the Old Testament, always in conjunction with the people of Israel. (See, for example, Daniel 12:1; Deuteronomy 29:18-20.) The scroll was kept in the Temple and contained the registry of the lineage for Israelites.

> ### Trail Marker #11
> ### Those of the synagogue of Satan (3:9)

To the ecclesia in Philadelphia ...

I am aware of your acts and have granted an open door before you that no one is able to lock. Those of the synagogue of Satan who are saying they are Jews and are not, they will be arriving and worshiping before your feet. They will know that I love you.

Notice that those "of the synagogue of Satan" are not lost forever.

Once the kingdom is restored with Christ reigning on the throne, those outside the city (including those "of the synagogue of Satan" as we see here) will enter to worship. And there they will see those of faithful Israel serving the King within the city.

> ## Trail Marker #12
> ## The seven letters (2:1 - 3:22)

Consider these seven letters directed to the seven ecclesias.

Notice that the audience is expected to be well versed in the Jewish history of the Old Testament; all that had been written to their fathers.

Each of the promises is conditioned; *to him that overcometh*. We find this same condition in the gospels and the Circumcision letters where faith plus works (enduring to the end) are requirements. But the concept is foreign to the language found in Paul's letters where salvation is by faith alone.

None of these promises can be realized by the Body of Christ, for they all fall into a sphere that is not pertinent to our expectation. Our expectation lies in the heavens, the celestial realm; but everything mentioned in these letters is concerned with an expectation in the kingdom to be restored upon the earth.

The difference between these letters and the New Testament epistles (letters) is significant!

It is impossible to see how these Revelation letters that are steeped in works could harmonize with the Body of Christ that is under grace and not law.

While many Bible translators use the word "church" when *ecclesia* occurs, it is important to remember that ecclesia simply means "out-called-ones." It is a group called-out from a larger group for a particular purpose. Each time the word appears it is important to review the context to determine the composition of the out-called-ones. And as we have seen, the ecclesia to whom these letters in Revelation are directed are Jewish believers, not the Body of Christ that we know to be "the church" today.

Throughout the Old Testament God's chosen people were the Israelites. With the Body of Christ removed from the scene in the end times, once again we see Israel assuming that role. Israel was not to be "calloused" forever, but only *UNTIL the complement of the nations may be entering.* (Romans 11:25) And then, as prophesied in Isaiah 59:20-21, the Rescuer will turn Israel away from her irreverence. (Romans 11:26)

> Trail Marker #13
> ## A door opens in heaven (4:1)

I saw a door open in heaven, and a voice as a trumpet said to me, Come up here and I will show you what must be occurring after these things. Immediately I came to be in spirit.

John is about to walk thru this door to perceive things that will occur in the Day of the Lord. He is made to be "in spirit," perhaps similar to the day he will receive an incorruptible body, but for now only temporarily. He is about to see events that are to take place in the future.

Milestones in Revelation *(Return of the King)*

++ Some observations along the way ++

In heaven John sees a throne and One sitting upon it. Elders were seated on 24 thrones around it.

Lightning and voices and thunder sounded out of the thrones, and the seven spirits of God were before the throne, as well as a glassy sea.

The visions John will describe alternate between heaven and earth. That which he sees on earth is the implementation of the vision he had previously seen in heaven.

Around the throne are four animals with eyes in front and behind, worshipping the Lord God Almighty. Their description matches that of the cherubim in Ezekiel 1:10.

Chapter 5. The One on the throne gives a scroll, sealed with seven seals, to the lamb who is worthy. From the description this would seem to be the title deed to the earth.

The Lamb appears to have been slain but was now standing. As it took the scroll those around worshipped, singing: *You are worthy to take the scroll and open the seals. You were slain and buy us with your blood. You make a kingdom and priesthood for our God out of every tribe and people and nation, and they shall be reigning on the earth.*

This kingdom and priesthood are comprised of Jews that have been scattered among the nations. Only those of Israel are ever referred to as a priesthood.

As the seals are removed from the title deed, we will see great repercussions upon the earth. The Lord is preparing to take possession of what is His.

Chapter 6. Seal #1 is opened. A rider on a white horse comes forth conquering. This corresponds with Matthew 24:5: *Many shall be coming in My name saying 'I am the Christ' and shall deceive many.*

This rider is not Christ, but a false Christ that conquers the nations to unite them against God. Many will believe this is the Messiah who will solve humanity's problems and usher in the millennium.

Seal #2 takes peace from the earth, that they should be slaying on another. Matthew 24:6 predicts they will hear of battles, with nation being roused against nation.

Seal #3 seems to speak of famine, which corresponds with Matthew 24:7 which predicts famines and quakes.

Seal #4 brings death, with jurisdiction over a fourth of the earth to kill with the blade and with famine and with wild beasts. This corresponds with Matthew 24:7b-8 which predicts death.

Seal #5 speaks of martyrs ... the souls of those who had been slain because of the word of God. They cry out for vengeance but are instructed to rest a little longer. Matthew 24:9 also predicts martyrs.

Cries for vengeance would seem to be completely foreign to the Body of Christ living in this current era of grace.

Seal #6 brings a great cataclysm, with the sun becoming black and the moon as blood and the stars falling from the sky. Mountains and islands are moved out of place. In Matthew 24:10-13 chaos was predicted.

The sun turning black had been foretold in Joel 2:30-31; Zephaniah 1:15; Isaiah 13:9-10; and Isaiah 34:4. Joel had foretold that before the great and terrible Day of the Lord the sun would be turned to darkness and the moon to blood. (Joel 2:31; Acts 2:20)

Paul had reported that a day of indignation would come. (Romans 2:5) The events of that day are now being shared with John.

Consider Matthew 24:30. The Son of Man appears immediately after this great cataclysm.

The sixth seal takes us to the same point as the seventh trumpet we will read of in chapter 11. So, the visions to follow are a review of the period already covered by these seals, with additional details provided and from a different perspective.

Trail Marker #14
The 144,000 (7:2)

A messenger instructs that none should be injured until the slaves of God are sealed on their foreheads. 144,000 are to be sealed out of every tribe of the sons of Israel; 12,000 of each of the 12 tribes.

There has been much speculation as to the identity of these 144,000. Despite the fact that each of the 12 tribes of Israel are named, the most popular interpretation is that the 144,000 represents the church.

But what we see here is God securing the remnant of Israel in the midst of the judgments and persecutions taking place during the Great Tribulation.

As for the seal upon their heads, it is interesting that the Romans marked their soldiers on the hand, and their servants on the forehead.

++ Some observations along the way ++

Meanwhile, in heaven ... Johns sees a multitude standing before the throne dressed in white robes, worshipping. He is told that these are the ones coming out of the great affliction.

Chapter 8. Seal #7 is opened and there is a hush in heaven. Seven trumpets are given to the seven messengers standing before God.

Another messenger casts fire to the earth with a golden thurible, and thunder and voices and lightning and an earthquake occur.

This seventh seal would seem to cover the entire period of judgment in the trumpets and vials we will read about thru Revelation 18:24, which will then be followed immediately by the coming of the Son of Man.

THE TRUMPETS (8:6)

Trumpet #1. Hail and fire mixed with blood are cast into the earth and a third of the earth is burned up. All green grass is burned up.

The trumpet judgments parallel the plagues in Egypt. The first plague was the turning of the waters into blood (Exodus 7:14-25).

Trumpet #2. A huge mountain burning with fire is cast into the sea. A third of the sea becomes blood, and a third of the sea creatures having a soul die. A third of the ships decay.

Trumpet #3. A large burning star falls out of heaven upon a third of the rivers and springs of water. A third of the waters become bitter, and many of mankind die of the waters.

Trumpet #4. A third of the sun and moon and stars are eclipsed and darkened.

Chapter 9. Trumpet #5. A star falls to the earth out of heaven, with the key of the well of the submerged chaos. Out of the well come fumes that darken the sun and air, and locusts that are as scorpions. They are instructed not to injure the grass or tree or any green thing; but only those of mankind that do not have God's seal on their foreheads. They are not to kill, but torment for five months. Men will seek death but not find it.

Trumpet #6. The four messengers bound at the river Euphrates are loosed. A third of mankind are killed. The remainder of mankind do not repent of their acts; worshipping demons and idols, murder, enchantments, prostitution, and theft.

Chapter 10. A messenger descends out of heaven, holding a tiny open scroll. As he cries out, with his right foot on the sea and his left foot on the land, the seven thunders speak. But John was told to seal that which the seven thunders spoke and not to record these things.

God instructs John as to how much of what he sees is to be revealed to mankind. Our curious nature wants to know all details about everything, but God is in control over what is revealed to us.

The messenger proclaims that there will be no further delay, and when the seventh messenger trumpets the secret of God is consummated.

> ### Trail Marker #15
> ## The 42 months (11:1-2)

I was told to measure the temple of God and the altar and those worshiping in it; but not the court outside the temple for it was given to the nations, and they will be treading the holy city for 42 months.

Where could we possibly see the Church, with these references to the temple, the altar, and the court of the Gentiles?

In Ezekiel 40-41 and Zechariah 2:1-3 measurements were made to claim ownership. The outer court is omitted because it was left to be trodden by the nations until the coming of Christ.

This 42-month period probably corresponds to the last half (3-1/2 years) of Daniel's 70th heptad. (Daniel 9:27) He tells of a prince that would come, making a treaty with the majority of the Jews, breaking the treaty after 3-1/2 years.

THE TWO WITNESSES (11:3)

Two witnesses will prophesy 1260 days clothed in sackcloth. Anyone wanting to injure them must be killed. Fire will issue from their mouth and devour their enemies.

They have authority to withhold rain, to turn the waters to blood, and to smite the land with every calamity.

When they finish their testimony the wild beast will kill them. The people will see their corpses on display for 3 ½ days and will rejoice, since these prophets tormented them.

After 3 ½ days the spirit of life out of God will enter into them and they will stand. Great fear will fall upon those observing. And as they are observed the two will ascend into heaven in a cloud.

In that hour a great earthquake will occur. A tenth of the city will fall and 7000 men will be killed.

> ### Trail Marker #16
> ## The seventh trumpet (11:15)

Trumpet #7. Loud voices in heaven say, *The kingdom of this world became our Lord's and His Christ's, and He shall be reigning for the eons of the eons.*

The seventh trumpet is the crisis of human history. Man's day is ending. The sovereignty over the earth passes from man, the instrument of Satan, to the Son of Man. The trumpet is the proclamation of the coming coronation of the rightful king of earth.

This seventh trumpet is not *the last trump* that we see in 1 Thessalonians 4:13ff. It is but the last in this *series* of seven trumpets. Every time a trumpet is blown there is a last trump or a final blast.

The seventh trumpet is sounded by a messenger. When the Lord comes for those in Christ (1 Thessalonians 4:16) He will descend from heaven with the shout of command and with the trumpet of God. This trumpet will be sounded by THE messenger, the Lord Himself, and not another. He is the Chief Messenger, and only His voice can wake the dead. He will be trumpeting. (1 Corinthians 15:52)

Even the seventh trumpet which ushers in the kingdom here in Revelation is not the last time a trumpet will sound. In the temple ritual and festivals the redeemed earth will again hear the trumpet. The seventh is the last in the *series* sounded here.

Furthermore, nothing we read here in association with the seventh trumpet is consistent with what we see at the last trump in 1 Thessalonians 4. The kingdom ushered in by the seventh trumpet is the sovereignty of Israel over the nations. The Body of Christ has no place in this! Furthermore, at this seventh blast the Lord does not descend to the earth, the kingdom is not setup, and no judgment of the nations follows. No dead are raised, no living ones are changed from a terrestrial body to a celestial one.

The seven trumpets deal with the nations, or gentiles who have taken political possession of the earth; not the Body of Christ.

> Trail Marker #17
> ## He will reign forever? (11:15)

The kingdom of this world became our Lord's and His Christ's, and He shall be reigning for the eons of the eons.

He will not reign *forever and ever* for we are told Christ will reign <u>until</u> all is subjected to Him (1 Corinthians 15:25), at which point He will subject Himself to God the Father and cease reigning.

He will reign *for the eons of the eons;* at least two eons (periods of time) out of all of the eons.

Milestones in Revelation *(Return of the King)*

++ Some observations along the way ++

The nations are angered. His indignation and the era for judging has come.

The temple in heaven is opened, and in it is the ark of God's covenant. Lightnings and voices and thunders and an earthquake and great hail occur.

This "temple section" covers the same era as the previous section. Both end with the establishing of Christ's kingdom, both share information on the 144,000 (7:4 and 14:1) and the wild beast (11:7; 13:1). But now these things are considered from a different perspective.

The previous section began with a vision of the throne, signifying political dominion. This section begins with a vision of the temple, signifying worship. It is now the era of world-wide worship of God, and the world must be rid of false religions and philosophies.

THE WOMAN AND THE DRAGON (12:1)

A great sign is seen in heaven; a woman clothed with the sun, with the moon under her feet, and a wreath of twelve stars on her head. She is pregnant and is crying, travailing and tormented to be bringing forth.

Another *sign* in heaven; a great fiery dragon with seven heads and ten horns and with diadems on each head. Its tail drags a third of the stars from heaven and casts them to the earth.

So a third of the angels cast their lot with the Adversary. The seven heads and ten horns picture the confederacy led by Satan that will control the earth in the end times.

The dragon stands before the woman waiting to devour her child when she brings it forth.

Trail Marker #18

The Adversary

Where is Satan ... the Adversary?

The common notion is that Satan is presiding in "hell." But until the end times he has access to heaven and earth, as in the days of Job.

As a dragon he is in heaven, and then comes to the earth. Later we find him back in heaven, battling with Michael. Michael and his messengers eject him from the heavens.

Later still he is chained in the abyss for 1000 years (20:12) before reappearing on the earth briefly. (20:7-9) Then he is cast into the lake of fire for the eons. (20:10)

Satan once used Herod in attempting to kill the child Jesus. Satan's objective was once to destroy the entire male line, making the birth of the seed of the woman impossible. Jehoram slew all his brethren so the royal line was reduced to one; him (2 Chronicles 21:4). But he had children, and Ahaziah was later the only lineal descendent of the royal line.

She had children, but all were killed by Athaliah; except one that escaped his fate. And in the book of Esther an attempt was made to destroy the entire nation. Now, in Revelation, Satan will try once again to destroy Israel.

Today the dragon is the true ruler of the nations. The dragon is the antithesis of the gentle and harmless lambkin. It is a picture of evil; representing Satan's character and activities in the end times.

But when confronting Eve in the Garden of Eden, Satan did not appear as a dragon. He did not wish to cause fear; but confidence.

Satan sometimes appears as <u>an angel of light</u> (2 Corinthians 11:14), but at other times he is as <u>a roaring lion</u> (1 Peter 5:8). He changes in appearance to suit the occasion. Here he assumes the role of a dragon, leaving behind the disguise of a deceiver to become the ferocious adversary.

Milestones in Revelation *(Return of the King)*

++ Some observations along the way ++

The woman brings forth a son who will shepherd all the nations with an iron club. The child is snatched away to God and to His throne.

The woman flees into the wilderness, to a place made ready by God, for her to be nourished for 1260 days.

Our Lord foretold the woman's flight in Matthew 24:15-22 and Mark 13:14-20. All in Judea are warned to flee to the mountains with great haste. The woman would appear to represent Israel which gave birth to the child (Christ) who was resurrected and ascended into heaven.

There is a battle in heaven. Michael and his messengers battle with the dragon and its messengers, who are cast out of heaven. (Daniel 12:1 also speaks of this battle.)

A loud voice in heaven warns: Woe to the land and sea, for the Adversary descended to you having great fury, being aware that his season is brief.

When the dragon is cast to the earth it persecutes the woman who brought forth the son. The woman is given two wings as a large vulture, that she may fly into the wilderness to the place made ready where she will be nourished a season, and seasons, and half a season, from the serpent's face.

We see once again this 3 ½ year period (42 months; 1260 days). This would be the last half of the final 7 year period, when the persecution of the faithful of Israel is ferocious. (Compare this with Matthew 24:16 and Daniel 9:27.)

The serpent is angry when the woman is protected, and comes away to do battle with the rest of her seed who are keeping the precepts of God and who have the testimony of Jesus.

> **Trail Marker #19**
> # Daniel 7-12

A consideration of the final six chapters of Daniel can shed light on our walk thru Revelation. Daniel lived from 605-530 BC, and he wrote his account while exiled in Babylonia after the defeat of Judah.

Much of this portion of Daniel focuses on wars between nations. And much of what Daniel sees would seem to have been fulfilled in history.

But some events Daniel speaks of continue to await fulfillment (at least in my opinion after studying these Scriptures for many years).

And while these struggles between nations appears to be the focus of Daniel's visions, what is really in view would appear to be the "world religions" which were always closely aligned with the nations.

So while "ten horns" might represent ten nations ... and while many commentators like to identify the nations that are in prophetic view ... it is really the world religions that are behind the nations that is in view. Nations and political powers rise and fall, but four religion-groups (Islam, Buddhism, Hinduism, and Judaism/Christianity) remain constant.

In Daniel the four beasts are distinct from one another, as are the world religions today (for the most part). But in Revelation we will see them merged into one world religion ... compliments of "the beast."

Besides the religions and nations, Daniel sees "a horn" arise that is a single personality ... one with a mouth declaring monstrous things and making war with the saints. (7:8) He is successful with his war on the saints until "The Transferror of Days" arrives ... when *the stated time* comes and *adjudication* is granted to the saints. (7:21)

Daniel tells us the ten horns represent ten kings that will arise, and that one will arise after them that will make declarations against the Supreme. He will success for *a season and two seasons and half a season.* (Again we see the 3 ½ year period.) But then his authority will pass away.

Much within Daniel's visions did find fulfillment in times now past. But some events are still awaiting fulfillment.

One example ... the historian Josephus finds fulfillment in the exploits of Antiochus Epiphanes, some 408 years after Daniel's prophecy. Antiochus was determined to unify his kingdom both religiously and socially, and he led a brutal suppression of Jewish worship. In 168 BC he seized Jerusalem on the Sabbath, erected an idol of Zeus, and desecrated the altar by offering a swine on it. This became known to the Jews as the abomination of desolation.

Antiochus died in 164 BC, and a year later Judas Maccabaeus rededicated the Jerusalem temple and re-started the daily sacrifices; 3 years and 55 days after Antiochus had abolished all sacrifices. Today this is celebrated as Hanukkah.

But the words of Jesus show that Daniel's prophecy was not entirely fulfilled. Despite what Antiochus had done, Jesus speaks of "the abomination of desolation" as a future event (Matthew 24:15). Antiochus Epiphanes was just a shadow of that which is to come.

It is not uncommon for prophecy to find a <u>partial</u> fulfillment in the short term, and an <u>ultimate</u> fulfillment later. An example would be the virgin who was to give birth to a child (Isaiah 7:14 and Matthew 1:23); fulfilled in Old Testament times but ultimately fulfilled by Christ. We know there was a short-term fulfillment, for Isaiah was providing a *sign* to Ahaz. This would not have been a *sign to Ahaz* had a virgin not given birth in that day. Still, the short-term fulfillment was only partial. The ultimate fulfillment arrived with the birth of Christ.

Milestones in Revelation (Return of the King)

> **Trail Marker #20**
> **Daniel's 70-7's** (Daniel 9:21)

One portion in Daniel will be very helpful to our understanding of Revelation.

Seventy sevens are segregated for your people and for your holy city; to detain transgression, to make sin come to end, to make a propitiatory shelter for depravity, to bring the righteousness of the eons, to seal the vision and the prophetic word, to anoint the holy of holies. (9:24)

From the going forth of the word to cause a return and to rebuild Jerusalem; from then until Messiah the Governor is 7-sevens and 62-sevens. After the 62-sevens, Messiah shall be cut off, and there will be no adjudication for Him. The city and the holy place shall be laid in ruins, with the other governor's coming. (9:25)

The events of this prophecy commence with the decree to rebuild Jerusalem. The rebuilding takes place after the initial 7-sevens (49 years). After another 62-sevens (434 years) Messiah comes, but He is "cut off" (crucified).

A pause takes place due to Israel's rebellion, leading to Paul's commissioning to gather the Body of Christ. The final "seven" (7 years) continues to await fulfillment.

But the hardening of Israel will come to an end (Romans 11:25) once God has fulfilled His purposes, after which the Body of Christ will be removed from the scene to fulfill its destiny in the heavens (1 Thessalonians 4), and the final 7-year period as described in Revelation will take place.

This rejection of the kingdom and the king was not seen by Daniel, and accounts for the lengthening of time (a pause) between the 69th seven and the final seven.

Back to Daniel ...

He will be master of a covenant with many for 1-seven. At half of the 7 he shall cause to cease the sacrifice and the approach present. On a wing of the sanctuary shall be desolating abominations. (9:27)

So, the final 7-year period is divided in half. A covenant to allow the restoration of Israel's temple worship is interrupted at the 3 1/2-year mark; unleashing the severe persecution and calamities in the final 3 1/2 years prior to the Lord's return.

Returning to Daniel, Gabriel is speaking ...

I have come to make you understand what shall befall your people in the latter days; for the vision is for future days. Then I shall return to fight with the chief of the kingdom of Persia. (10:14)

"Your people" would be Daniel's people ... Israel. So again we see that these end time events are centered upon Israel ... not "the church."

An era of distress will come to pass such as has not occurred since there was a nation on the earth. (12:1)

It is for an appointed time, two appointed times and half an appointed time. (12:7)

*From the era when the continuous ritual is taken away, and to the setting of the abomination of desolation, is **1290 days**. Happy is he who will tarry and attain to the **1335 days**. (12:11)*

The 3-½ years as mentioned throughout (the last half of the final seven) would be 1260 days. Here we see 1290 days.

It could be that the additional 30 day period is needed for the priesthood to make the necessary arrangements to restore the true worship of God. And the additional 45 days (bringing the total to 1335 mentioned here) could be for the benefit of Daniel and others who had died and who awaited the resurrection ("the former resurrection"). Once all is ready within the kingdom it would be time for their rousing.

Now returning to Revelation ...

Chapter 13. THE BEAST.

As the dragon stands by the sea a wild beast ascends out of the sea, having ten horns and seven heads, with diadems and blasphemous names on its heads.

The dragon gives the beast its power and throne and great authority.

Now that the dragon has been cast down to earth, it proceeds to make war with the woman and her seed. The first step is to introduce the beast.

One of the beast's heads appeared as if slain, and then cured. The whole earth marvels after the beast.

So at least to all appearances Satan has brought back to life one that had been killed.

It would seem that the beast is filled with charisma, and promising peace and happiness. Many within religious circles today announce the coming of a great revival to sweep the earth, introducing the kingdom with peace and happiness. Could it be that religion itself (Christendom) is playing into Satan's hand, preparing the way for the man of sin to be introduced and embraced?

Scripture tells us that as we near the end times conditions will get worse. Many today are proclaiming a different message, stating that conditions will get better as the gospel spreads across the land.

They worship the dragon, seeing that it gives authority to the wild beast. They worship the wild beast saying, Who is able to battle with it?

The beast speaks great things and blasphemies. It is given authority to do its will for 42 months. It blasphemes God's name and His tabernacle and those tabernacling in heaven.

Again we see the 3 ½ year period (42 months). In the middle of the seven year period the beast will break his covenant with Israel and make ware against the saints (Daniel 9:27).

The beast is given to do battle with the saints and to conquer them. Authority is given to it over every tribe and people and language and nation. All who dwell on the earth will worship it, everyone whose name is not written in the scroll of life. Here is the endurance and faith of the saints.

Chapter 13. ANOTHER BEAST.

Another beast ascends out of the land. It exercises all the authority of the first beast, making everyone worship the first beast.

It does great signs, deceiving. Whoever does not worship the image of the beast is killed.

We should note that miracles are not evidence or proof of divine or righteous activity. A belief that this is so will play a big part in Satan's ability to deceive.

It causes all to have an emblem on their right hand or forehead, and no one is able to buy or sell unless they have this emblem of the wild beast, or its name, or the number of its name. The number is the number of mankind; ***666.***

History has never seen myriads receive the emblem, name or number of the wild beast. No religion has had so many followers enlist within such a short span of time. Clearly these events continue to await fulfillment in the future.

Most within Israel are safe and nourished, having taken the emblem. But war is being waged upon the faithful remnant. The faithful cannot buy or sell due to this embargo, and they are now totally dependent upon God for provision; reminiscent of the days in the wilderness.

Notice that there is no provision found in Revelation for the protection of the Body of Christ among the nations. Only ISRAEL is addressed. The Body of Christ is not mentioned because it is not present when these things occur.

Today, in the 21st Century, the Day of the Lord is imminent; but the coming of Christ for the Body is even MORE imminent.

Now, back to heaven …

Chapter 14. THE EONIAN EVANGEL.

*I saw the Lambkin standing on mount Zion with **144,000** having its name and its Father's name written on their foreheads.*

A messenger is flying in heaven having an eonian evangel to bring to those on the earth; to every nation and tribe and language and people.

"Be afraid of God and give glory to Him, for the hour of His judging came. Worship the Maker of heaven and the land and the sea and the springs of water."

In Matthew 24:14 we were told the *evangel* would be proclaimed worldwide as a testimony to the nations, before the end would come.

This *eonian evangel* is not for our current day. It is for the time noted here in Revelation; a time of judgement; not grace. It does not ask mankind to *believe*. It tells men to *fear* God, and it demands that only God is to be worshipped; the One Who created the universe! So, this is an evangel of fear, with the hour of judgment having come.

The eonian evangel is a very basic message, with no mention of Christ's blood and redemption. Worship is demanded solely on the basis of His being the Creator. This tells us of the awful state of the earth in these days, where such a primitive evangel is needed.

Milestones in Revelation *(Return of the King)*

Chapter 14. BABYLON, AND THE HARVEST.

A second messenger proclaims the fall of Babylon, which had made all nations partake of her prostitution.

A third messenger warns that anyone worshiping the wild beast and its image and taking its emblem is also drinking of God's fury and indignation, and he will be tormented in fire and Sulphur.

The fumes of the torment are ascending <u>for the eons of the eons</u>. This would be the last two eons, as compared with all of the eons described in the Scriptures. But these last two eons, too, will end; for an eon is not of endless duration.

One like a son of mankind is seen on a white cloud, with a sharp sickle. The hour had come, and He cast His sickle on the earth and reaped.

Chapter 15. Another sign in heaven ... seven messengers having the last seven calamities. Each of the seven messengers has a golden bowl brimming with God's fury.

Chapter 16. THE BOWLS.

Bowl #1. Malignant ulcers on all who have the beast's emblem and who worship its image.

Bowl #2. The sea becomes blood, and every living thing in the sea dies.

Bowl #3. The rivers and springs become as blood.

Bowl #4. The sun is given to scorch mankind with fire and heat. They do not repent and give Him glory.

Bowl #5. The beast's kingdom becomes dark and they are in misery. They blaspheme God for their miseries and do not repent.

Bowl #6. The Euphrates is dried up, making ready for the kings from the orient to cross.

Out of the mouths of the dragon, the wild beast, and the false prophet come three unclean spirits, doing signs and going out to the kings of the inhabited earth to mobilize them for the battle of the great day of God Almighty.

They are mobilized at the place called, in Hebrew, Armageddeon. Armageddon (or *har-megiddo*) is "the mount of Megiddo."

Bowl #7. Lightnings and voices and thunder, and a great earthquake such as did not occur since mankind came to be on the earth.

The great city (Babylon) is divided into three parts, and the cities of the nations fall.

Babylon the great is given the cup of the fury of God's indignation.

Every island flees, and the mountains are not found.

Large hail descends upon mankind, and men blaspheme God because of this hail.

Chapter 17. THE WOMAN ON THE BEAST.

A woman, "the great prostitute," had committed prostitution with the kings of the earth. (Verse 18 tells us this woman is a city.)

On her forehead was written: Secret. Babylon the Great, the mother of the prostitutes and the abominations of the earth. The woman was drunk with the blood of the saints and the witnesses of Jesus.

Ten kings are obtaining authority one hour with the beast. They are united and are giving their power and authority to the wild beast.

They will battle with the Lambkin, and the Lambkin will conquer them; as It is Lord of lords and King of kings.

Chapter 18. THE FALL OF BABYLON

A messenger descends and cries loudly, It falls! Babylon the great! Because of her prostitution all the nations have fallen.

The kings of the earth commit prostitution with her, and the merchants of the earth are rich because of her power to indulge.

Commerce today controls the world. This was not so in Rome, which was a military dictatorship. Commerce had not yet been developed.

Some would say this is an accurate description of the USA; wielding broad financial influence around the world and degrading into many sorts of ungodly behavior. While this may be true, we cannot say this passage is prophetically speaking of the USA.

BUT; we can learn from these words and understand that which God despises. This should cause us to seek from God's Word those behaviors and acts that He approves of, and those He does not. It is not that we are trying to earn His favor or our salvation, but because of His grace it is simply the right thing to do; the appropriate response on our part.

The kings of the earth who commit prostitution and indulge with her will lament and grieve over her when they see the smoke of her burning, standing afar off for fear of her torment. They will say, Woe that great city. Babylon the strong city. For in one hour your judging came.

The merchants of the earth lament and mourn over her, for no one is buying their cargo any longer.

> Trail Marker #21
>
> ## The Bride (19:6-7)

Chapter 19. In heaven there is worship, for the just judging of God had come. And the wedding of the Lambkin came, and Its bride makes herself ready.

Israel is often referred to as the bride of Jehovah. He became her husband at Sinai. (Jeremiah 31:22) But she forsook Him to pursue other lovers. (Hosea 2:6-13) So He gave her a bill of divorce. (Deuteronomy 24:1-4)

Sent into captivity Israel could never be His again according to the law. But nonetheless He invites her to return. (Jeremiah 3:1) He promises to wait for her and to keep her for Himself until the latter days. (Hosea 3:3)

During the Lord's earthly ministry He called Israel a wicked and adulterous generation, for they had forsaken God.

How can this be the Church that has made herself ready? Members of the Body of Christ are already made ready (Colossians 1:12). God has made us ready and we are complete in Him (Colossians 2:10). We cannot be more ready than how He Himself has made us.

We are His BODY, not His Bride. Israel is His BRIDE.

The marriage is a resuming of God's relationship with Israel.

> ## Trail Marker #22
> ## The return of the King (19:11)

I saw heaven open and a white horse. The One sitting on it is called Faithful and True. In righteousness He is judging and battling. He wears a cloak dipped in blood, and His name is called The Word of God.

Remember the white horse of the false christ in 6:2. It is now time for the white horse bearing the true Christ to appear.

The armies in heaven follow Him on white horses. Out of His mouth a sharp blade is issuing, that with it He should be smiting the nations. And He will be shepherding with an iron club.

He is treading the wine trough of the fury of God's indignation. And on His cloak and on His thigh a name is written: King of kings and Lord of lords.

The wild beast and the kings of the earth and their armies gathered to do battle with Him.

The beast and the false prophet are arrested and cast living into the lake of fire burning with Sulphur. The rest were killed with the blade coming out of His mouth.

The beast and false prophet cannot be killed as mere men. They remain alive in the lake of fire at the close of the 1000 years. The armies are mortal and are slain, and their bodies are eaten by the birds of the air.

And so the battle is short. Who can withstand the power of God?

Milestones in Revelation *(Return of the King)*

> ### Trail Marker #23
> ### The 1000 years ^(20:1)

*A messenger descends with the key of the submerged chaos and a large chain. He binds the dragon, the ancient serpent who is the Adversary and Satan, for **1000** years; casting him into the submerged chaos, locking it, and sealing it, lest he should still deceive the nations before the **1000** years is finished. Afterwards he must be loosed for a little time.*

I saw thrones, and judgment was granted to those seated on them.

In Matthew 19:28 we were told of apostles on these thrones. And Matthew 25:31-46 foretells this judgement.

*The souls of those executed because of the testimony of Jesus and the word of God, and those who do not worship the beast or its image or take the emblem, they also live and reign with Christ **1000** years. This is the former resurrection. The rest of the dead do not live until the **1000** years is finished.*

The Body of Christ is not found in this resurrection or reigning, for they were resurrected to life before the events of Revelation commenced. The Body reigns in the heavens, judging messengers (1 Corinthians 6:3) while the resurrected Bride-Israel reigns upon the earth during this period.

*Happy are those having part in the former resurrection. The second death has no jurisdiction over them, and they will be priests of God and of Christ, reigning with Him the **1000** years.*

Bullinger summarizes the 1000 years as the absence of Satan, the restoration of the earth, many physical marvels, converting deserts into gardens, changes in the sun, moon, and stars that affect the climate and fruitfulness of the earth, changes in the nature and habits of the wild animals, righteous government, and prolonged life and improved health.

But despite all of the good, there is yet a final rebellion to come.

Trail Marker #24
The final rebellion (20:7)

*When the **1000** years is finished Satan will be loosed from his jail. He will come out to deceive all the nations in the four corners of the earth; Gog and Magog mobilizing for battle. Their number is as the sand of the sea. They went up over the breadth of the earth, surrounding the citadel of the saints and the beloved city.*

And fire descended from God out of heaven and devoured them.

Man has enjoyed 1000 years of God's goodness. The knowledge of His goodness has flooded the earth. Man would observe a righteous government; with peace and prosperity.

But these things cannot create a new heart. The carnal mind is at enmity with God and is not subject to the Law of God. So, when Satan is loosed man is quickly deceived and ready to believe his lies. For man to understand his weakness, Satan HAD to be loosed for a season.

The Adversary was cast into the lake of fire and sulphur where the beast and the false prophet were also. They will be tormented day and night <u>for the eons of the eons</u>.

Not "forever and ever" but for a finite period of time ... *the eons of the eons.* God can surely not become ALL IN ALL (1 Corinthians 15:28) until even these creatures bow before Him and this second death is abolished.

Milestones in Revelation *(Return of the King)*

> Trail Marker #25
> # The judgment (20:11)

I saw a great white throne, and He Who was seated upon it was the One from Whose face earth and heaven fled. I saw the dead, the great and small, standing before the throne. Scrolls were opened. And another scroll was opened which was the scroll of life. The dead were judged by that which is written in the scrolls in accord with their acts.

Notice that this judgement is based upon acts, not faith. Paul's message was justification by faith alone, lest any should boast. That was the message of grace entrusted to him and proclaimed to the Body of Christ. But now, in Revelation when Christ returns to the earth, judgment is based upon acts.

In God's Word, judgment is not simply the punishment for crime. It is the bringing of justice; the righting of wrongs. Secrets will be exposed, scores settled, and each will receive his due. All will recognize the injustices that took place, and all things will be put right. All will acknowledge God's wisdom and justice, and every knee will bow.

The sea gives up the dead in it, and death and the unseen give up the dead in them. They are condemned, each in accord with their acts. Death and the unseen are cast into the lake of fire. This is the second death; the lake of fire. If anyone is not found written in the scroll of life, he is cast into the lake of fire.

The scroll of life is specific to Israel. Moses seems to have referred to it when he asks to be blotted out of God's book to save the sinners within Israel (Exodus 32:32). We learned that the conquerors will not have their names erased from the scroll of life (3:5). But those who are not conquerors but who worship the wild beast are not written in the scroll of life (13:8).

Daniel, who speaks of Israel, says those written in the scroll will be delivered (Daniel 12:1). And Paul seems to say that it was his fellow workers of the Circumcision whose names are in the scroll of life (Philippians 4:3).

So, this scroll is not a listing of ALL who receive life in this present age of grace. It is specific to ISRAEL where salvation comes thru a mixture of grace and works, and where one's name could be erased based on wrong conduct.

So, the lake of fire now contains everyone, those living at the time and the dead which are raised for judgment. The only exception would be those whose names were written in the book of life, and the Body of Christ which had previously been "changed" (if living) or resurrected (if dead) to meet the Lord in the air (1 Thessalonians 4:13ff).

It is interesting that the only *duration* described for the lake of fire is for Satan, the beast, and the false prophet who will remain there *for the eons of the eons*. Not so with all others. We see they are cast into the lake of fire, but for how long? However long God determines is appropriate and necessary.

Lastly ... the lake of fire is described as "the second death." Ultimately death (and therefore the lake of fire) will be abolished (1 Corinthians 15:21-28). The lake of fire is a part of God's process in leading all of His creation to reconciliation.

Trail Marker #26
The New Jerusalem (21:1)

I saw a new heaven and a new earth, for the former heaven and the former earth pass away, and the sea is no more. And I saw the holy city, new Jerusalem, descending out of heaven from God, made ready as a bride adorned for her husband.

We enter a new eon; the Day of God. 2 Peter 3:7-10 reports that the present heavens and earth will pass away with a booming noise, with the elements dissolved by combustion. The earth and the works in it will be burned up at the coming of the day of God. Isaiah 65:17 promised this new heaven and new earth that was to come.

And notice that the holy city is not heaven itself. It descends OUT OF heaven. The city is heavenly in character but is to be located upon the earth.

The tabernacle of God is with mankind, and He will be tabernacling with them. They will be His peoples, and God Himself will be with them.

He will be brushing away every tear from their eyes. Death will be no more, nor mourning, nor clamor, nor misery. For the former things have passed away.

This is foretold in Isaiah 65:17-19.

I am making all new! I have become the Alpha and the Omega, the Origin and the Consummation.

He who is conquering shall be enjoying this allotment. I will be a God to him and he will be a son to Me.

But the timid, the unbelievers, the abominable, murderers, paramours, enchanters, idolaters, and all the false – their part is in the lake burning with fire and Sulphur; the second death. (21:8)

> ## Trail Marker #27
> ## What is the lake of fire?

Some contend it must be a death just like the first, where one has no consciousness.

Others contend it is a figurative death, and that the lake of fire is a purging or a process that prepares the subject for life in God's kingdom.

Not much information is provided in Revelation as to these details, but we know enough that we certainly would want to avoid experiencing the second death.

And whatever the second death is it is not "forever and ever" but for a finite period of time. The end result is that God's will is accomplished. Every knee will bow, all will be subjected, all will be reconciled to God, and He will become All in all. (1 Corinthians 15:28)

> Trail Marker #28
> ## The holy city (21:10)

He carried me away, in spirit, on a high mountain and showed me the holy city, Jerusalem, as it descended out of heaven.

It had twelve portals, with twelve messengers at the portals with their names inscribed; which are <u>the names of the twelve tribes of the sons of Israel</u>.

The wall had twelve foundations, and on them were <u>the names of the twelve apostles</u> of the Lambkin.

The names of the twelve tribes and the twelve apostles shows us that this city is for Israel. The twelve have this high honor. Paul, the greatest apostle of them all, is not mentioned. Throughout Revelation ISRAEL is the focus; not the nations.

Paul introduced the Body of Christ with no wall or barrier between Jew and Gentile. But the new Jerusalem has nothing to do with the Body of Christ which has long since departed the earth.

There was no temple, for the Lord God Almighty is its temple, and the Lambkin. The city had no need of the sun or moon, for the glory of God illuminated it, and its lamp is the Lambkin.

The nations will walk by means of its light, and the kings of the earth will carry their glory into it. The portals will not be locked by day, and there will be no night there. They will carry the glory and the honor of the nations into it, but nothing contaminating, nor one who makes an abomination or lie will enter. Only those written in the Lambkin's scroll of life will enter.

Righteousness is implanted within the very being of the saints (Israel), but it must be enforced among the nations. Christ will rule with an iron club (Psalm 2:9). Men are still "free" to pursue the desires of their flesh, but there will be penalties for disobedience. While freed from the control of spiritual forces by the binding of Satan, the nations will still be influenced by their own inward corruption.

This, too, is a necessary part of God's plan, leading mankind to understand the need for dependence upon God. That is the function of God's government in this final era, administered by Israel.

To see what occurs AFTER this final era, refer to 1 Corinthians 15.

The saints in Israel will serve as priests for the millennial era. But in the new earth there is no temple. It is not that worship has ceased, but that which was outward will have become inward.

He showed me a river of water of life issuing out of the throne of God and the Lambkin. In the center of its square and on either side of the river was the log of life, producing twelve fruits in accord with each month. The leaves of the log are for the cure of the nations. (22:1)

The tree of life was first seen in Genesis 3:24. Here, in the final eon, we see it again. Those living do not have immortal bodies, but mortal; for the leaves are needed for their cure. If there was unfailing health, if sin was gone, and if the curse was removed, what would be the need for these leaves for *the cure of the nations?*

His slaves will offer divine service to Him. They will see His face, and His name will be on their foreheads. And they will be reigning <u>for the eons of the eons</u>.

So, the leaves of the tree are needed for the cure of the nations, government is still needed to rule, and the second death is still in operation. But as Revelation closes we do not yet see the final state of mankind.

Only to Paul was it revealed that which will take place after the conclusion of Revelation; when death is abolished; when every knee will bow; when all are subjected; when Christ has accomplished all that has been assigned to Him and when He turns over the throne to God the Father, and when God at last becomes All in all (1 Corinthians 15).

Trail Marker #29
Those outside (22:14-15)

Happy are those who are rinsing their robes, that it will be their license to the log of life, and they may be entering the portals into the city.

Outside are curs, enchanters, paramours, murderers, idolaters, and everyone fabricating and fondling falsehood. (22:15)

But were these not destroyed in the second death?

Compare 22:15 with 21:8. It seems that those "outside" (22:15) are those that are in the lake of fire (21:8). They are *outside* the holy city. Perhaps, then, the second death is a figurative death.

(A good book that explores this possibility is *"Journey to and through the Second Death"* by J. Phillip Scranton.)

++ Some closing thoughts ++

Revelation is not the final word. While it may occupy the final place in order in the Bible, there is more to follow the events recorded in Revelation. Even as Revelation concludes, mankind is a work in progress.

In his "Commentary on Revelation," E.W. Bullinger notes:

"What we have to look for now is not the conversion of the world, but the judgment of the world. The professing church is deceiving the world. It tells the world that its mission is to improve the world and, by improving its sanitation, housing its poor, and generally preaching the gospel of earthly citizenship, to bring on the millennium, in which no Christ is thought of or wanted!

While the majority of the Church's teachers are loudly proclaiming that "the day of the Lord" will not come till the world's conversion comes, the Spirit and truth of God are declaring that the day shall not come until the apostasy comes. (2 Thessalonians 2:3)

While the majority of the Church's teachers are maintaining that the world is not yet good enough for Christ, the Spirit is declaring in the Word that the world is not yet bad enough."

This overview contains the thoughts and opinions of the author, and is a work in progress as his study of the Scriptures continues. Some things that God has revealed are very clear. That Christ died for our sins; that He was entombed; and that He was roused (1 Corinthians 15:3) is clear. That all are to be ultimately reconciled to God thru the work of Christ is also very clear (1 Corinthians 15:20-28). But on many specifics in the Scriptures there are a variety of interpretations and opinions, and none should conclude they have the complete and final understanding on these matters that are less clear. The reader is encouraged to consider various opinions, but to study and to think for himself. Within the Body of Christ we should study and discuss our understandings so as to mutually reach a more complete understanding of that which God has revealed.

Unless otherwise noted, Scriptures are taken from the Concordant Literal New Testament and the Concordant Version of the Old Testament. Concordant Publishing Concern, 15570 West Knochaven Road, Santa Clarita, CA 91387 (www.Concordant.org)

Grace Evangel Fellowship:
P O Box 6, Wilmore, KY 40390
www.GraceEvangel.org

The Consummation

As Revelation comes to an end, we see the end of the ages. But as the last "Amen" of Revelation 22 is uttered, there is more to come. The crowning event of the ages is found in 1 Corinthians 15, the "consummation" of the ages. Many believe the end of Revelation is a description of the eternal heavens that we will experience when the resurrection takes place. But there are numerous reasons to conclude that this is not the case, and that 1 Corinthians 15 happens <u>after</u> the end of Revelation 22.

Revelation	1 Corinthians
The slaves of God are reigning (22:5) There are still "kings of the earth" (21:24)	All sovereignty, authority and power nullified (15:24)
Christ is seated on the throne (21:5)	Christ must reign UNTIL He places all enemies under His feet (15:25) When All is subject to Christ, He subjects Himself to God (15:28) All sovereignty, authority, power nullified (15:24)
Lake of fire (second death) still exists (21:8)	Last enemy (death) abolished (15:27)
Leaves on the tree for "the cure of the nations" implies corruptible bodies needing the leaves to sustain life (22:2)	Incorruptible, spiritual body (15:42-44)
Twelve tribes (21:12) Twelve apostles (21:14) Nations outside city (21:24)	No Jewish connotations in 1 Corinthians 15. No barrier between Jew and Greek in Paul's writings.
All speaks of a physical place upon the earth with mortal bodies; much like our present world but with Christ reigning and keeping evil out (22:14-15)	Paul describes a spiritual realm with no corruption, no reign, no power. All are subjected. There are no enemies, sin, or rebellion. The purpose of the ages has been achieved. God is All in all. (How could He be All in all with death, the enemy, still present?)
Revelation describes the final age/eon.	Paul describes "The Consummation" which occurs after the ages/eons have been completed.

In Revelation 21:1 John perceives "a new heaven and a new earth", and he sees "the holy city, new Jerusalem, descending <u>out of heaven</u>." The New Jerusalem is not heaven itself, but it descends <u>out of heaven</u>.

About the Author

Bob Evely is Vice President with a national company, overseeing sales, sales training, servicing, marketing, and special projects. He is a graduate of Oakland University (Rochester, Michigan) and has a Master of Divinity (M.Div.) Degree from Asbury Theological Seminary (Wilmore, Kentucky). For three and a half years Bob served as pastor of the Canton and West Point United Methodist Churches in Salem, Indiana; and for five years he served as pastor of the Open Door Free Methodist Church in Nicholasville, Kentucky. Both were bi-vocational positions, with Bob supporting his family through full time employment.

In May 2002 Bob resigned as pastor of Open Door Free Methodist Church to found Grace Evangel Fellowship, an independent ministry/church based in Wilmore, Kentucky. His ministry includes writing, speaking, teaching, and corresponding via email.

Bob resides in Wilmore, Kentucky with his wife Jill (since 1975). Originally from the Romeo, Michigan area the Evelys have five children: Cris (Jen), Dusty (Sharon), Chad (Molly), Kari (Jason), and Scott (Martha). As of this writing they are blessed with 7 grandchildren (Elinor, Allison, Abby, Lilli, Livi, Annabelle, and Alex).

Jill homeschooled all five children, and for 20 years represented Sonlight Curriculum as a consultant. Besides staying busy as a wife, mother, and grandma, Jill is an accomplished soap maker (PrairieKari.com) and she continues to encourage parents interested in homeschooling their children.

The author can be contacted at Grace Evangel Fellowship, P O Box 6, Wilmore, Kentucky 40390; or via email bob@GraceEvangel.org

Books by Bob Evely

At the End of the Ages; the Abolition of Hell (2002)

The Visitation; An Overview of the New Testament, Part One (2018)

The Waiting; An Overview of the New Testament, Part Two (2018)

The Pause; An Overview of the New Testament, Part Three (2018)

The Return of the King; An Overview of the New Testament, Part Four (2018)

Milestones in the New Testament (2018)

Many shorter writings can be found at GraceEvangel.org

Book Artists at Work
Allison, Elinor & Lilli Evely